Story by Kazutaka

Art by Kai Tomohiro

03

DESTINY LOVERS

CONTENTS

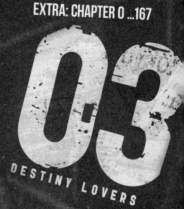

03

DESTINY LOVERS

CHAPTER 23: PLEASURE VS. COURAGE (1)

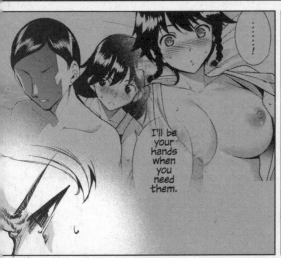

I'll be your hands when you need them.

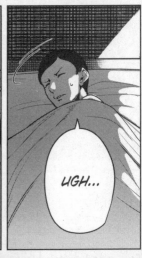

UGH...

WHAT'S WRONG WITH ME?

THESE EMOTIONS...

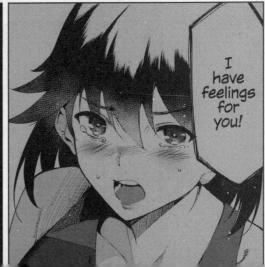

I have feelings for you!

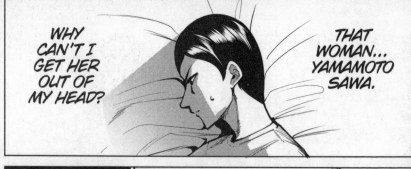

WHY CAN'T I GET HER OUT OF MY HEAD?

THAT WOMAN... YAMAMOTO SAWA.

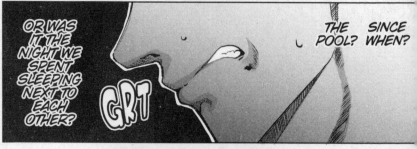

OR WAS IT THE NIGHT WE SPENT SLEEPING NEXT TO EACH OTHER?

GRT

THE POOL?

SINCE WHEN?

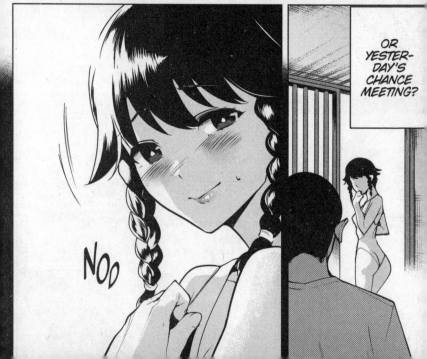

OR YESTER-DAY'S CHANCE MEETING?

NOD

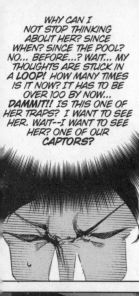 WHY CAN I NOT STOP THINKING ABOUT HER? SINCE WHEN? SINCE THE POOL? NO... BEFORE...? WAIT... MY THOUGHTS ARE STUCK IN A LOOP! HOW MANY TIMES IS IT NOW? IT HAS TO BE OVER 100 BY NOW... DAMMIT!! IS THIS ONE OF HER TRAPS? I WANT TO SEE HER. WAIT--I WANT TO SEE HER? ONE OF OUR **CAPTORS?**

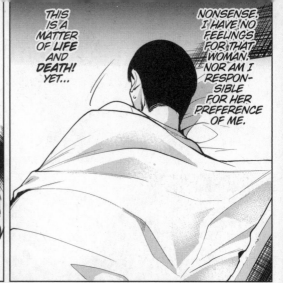 THIS IS A MATTER OF **LIFE** AND **DEATH!** YET...

NONSENSE. I HAVE NO FEELINGS FOR THAT WOMAN. NOR AM I RESPONSIBLE FOR HER PREFERENCE OF ME.

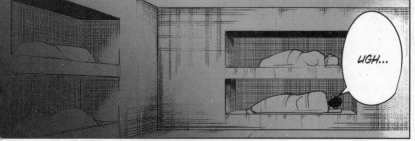 UGH...

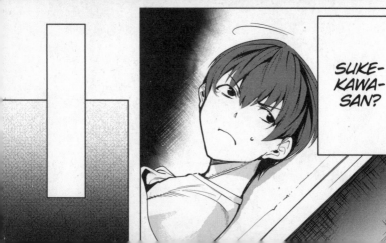 SUKE-KAWA-SAN?

THE NEXT DAY
BLAM
BLAM
BLAM
!!
HA! SO, YOU SOFT DICKS FINALLY SHOWED UP, HUH?
LET'S GET ONE THING STRAIGHT BEFORE WE GET STARTED. I'M NOT AS NICE AS MITSUKO.
SNUGGLING UP TOGETHER IN THE SAME BED? YOU CAN KISS THOSE DAYS GOODBYE.

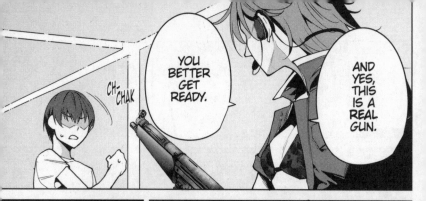

CH-CHAK

YOU BETTER GET READY.

AND YES, THIS IS A REAL GUN.

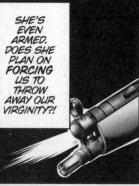

SHE'S EVEN ARMED. DOES SHE PLAN ON **FORCING** US TO THROW AWAY OUR **VIRGINITY?!**

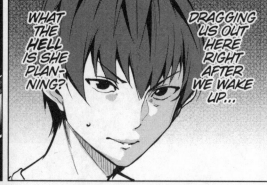

WHAT THE HELL IS SHE PLAN-NING?

DRAGGING US OUT HERE RIGHT AFTER WE WAKE UP...

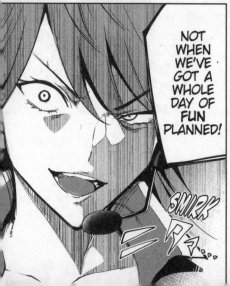

NOT WHEN WE'VE GOT A WHOLE DAY OF **FUN** PLANNED!

SMIRK

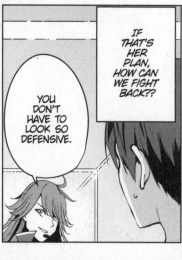

YOU DON'T HAVE TO LOOK SO DEFENSIVE.

IF THAT'S HER PLAN, HOW CAN WE FIGHT BACK??

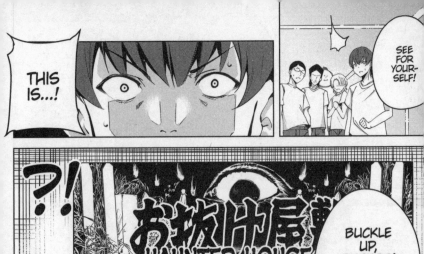

THIS IS...!

SEE FOR YOUR-SELF!

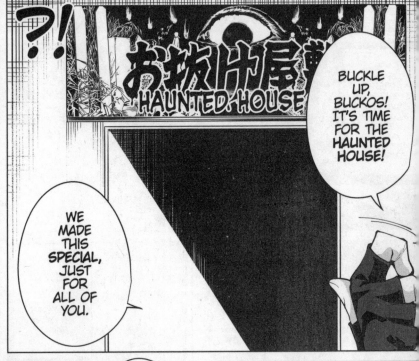

?!

お化け屋敷 HAUNTED HOUSE

BUCKLE UP, BUCKOS! IT'S TIME FOR THE HAUNTED HOUSE!

WE MADE THIS SPECIAL, JUST FOR ALL OF YOU.

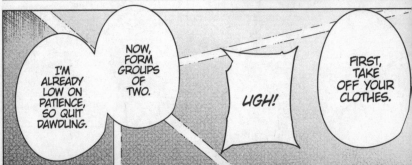

I'M ALREADY LOW ON PATIENCE, SO QUIT DAWDLING.

NOW, FORM GROUPS OF TWO.

UGH!

FIRST, TAKE OFF YOUR CLOTHES.

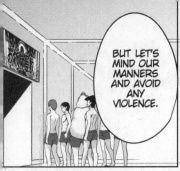

BUT LET'S MIND OUR MANNERS AND AVOID ANY VIOLENCE.

FUJISHIRO & SUKEKAWA

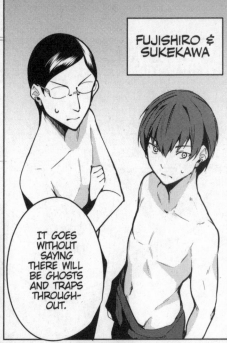

IT GOES WITHOUT SAYING THERE WILL BE GHOSTS AND TRAPS THROUGHOUT.

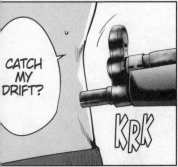

CATCH MY DRIFT?

KRK

ALL RIGHT! GET GOING!!

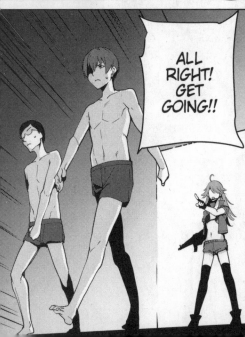

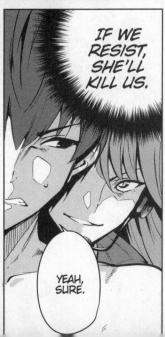

IF WE RESIST, SHE'LL KILL US.

YEAH, SURE.

THEY'RE IN.
HAUNTED HOUSE
Let the game begin.
ROGER THAT.

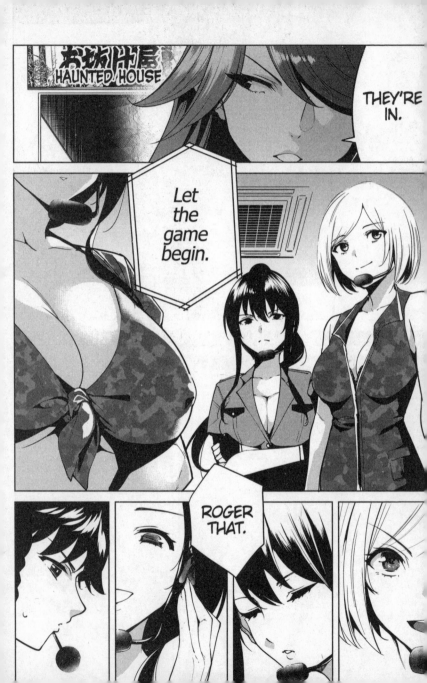

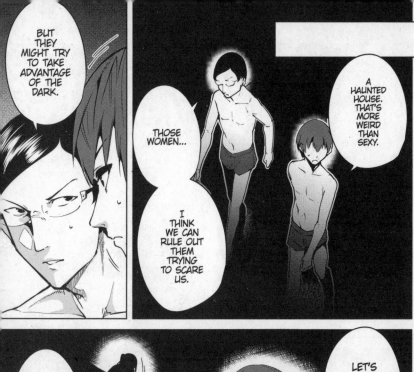

BUT THEY MIGHT TRY TO TAKE ADVANTAGE OF THE DARK.

A HAUNTED HOUSE. THAT'S MORE WEIRD THAN SEXY.

THOSE WOMEN...

I THINK WE CAN RULE OUT THEM TRYING TO SCARE US.

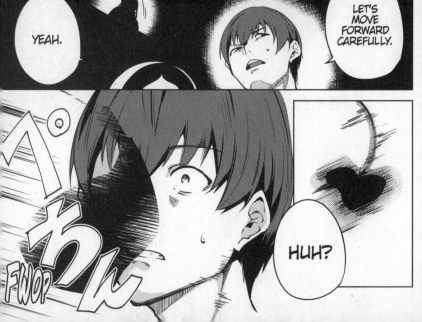

YEAH.

LET'S MOVE FORWARD CAREFULLY.

HUH?

FWOP

AHHHHH!!
WAHH!
S-SETTLE DOWN, FUJI-SHIRO-KUN!
IT'S JUST A PAIR OF...
PANTIES?

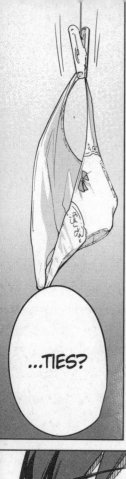

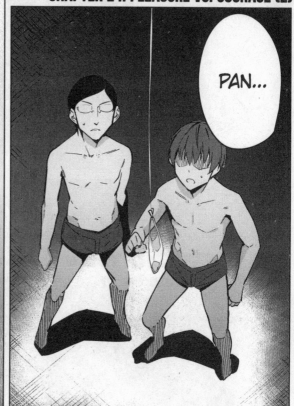

PAN...

...TIES?

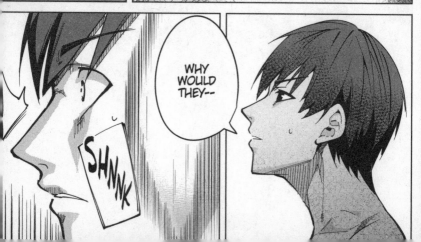

WHY WOULD THEY--

SHNNNK

DAMMIT, THESE PANTIES KEEP SCARING THE HELL OUTTA ME!!
FUJI-SHIRO-KUN... TAKE A GOOD LOOK AROUND.
AGAIN ?!
WHA ...?!
WE'RE SUR-ROUNDED...
BY PANTIES!!

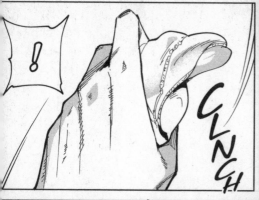

! CLNCH

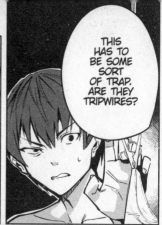

THIS HAS TO BE SOME SORT OF TRAP. ARE THEY TRIPWIRES?

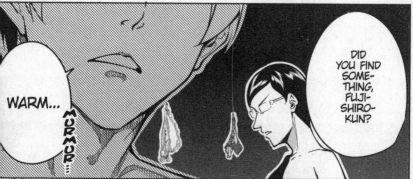

WARM...

MURMUR...

DID YOU FIND SOMETHING, FUJI-SHIRO-KUN?

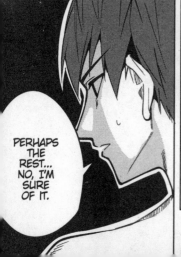

PERHAPS THE REST... NO, I'M SURE OF IT.

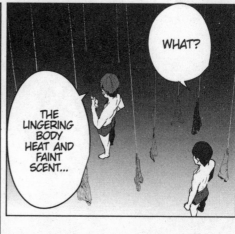

THE LINGERING BODY HEAT AND FAINT SCENT...

WHAT?

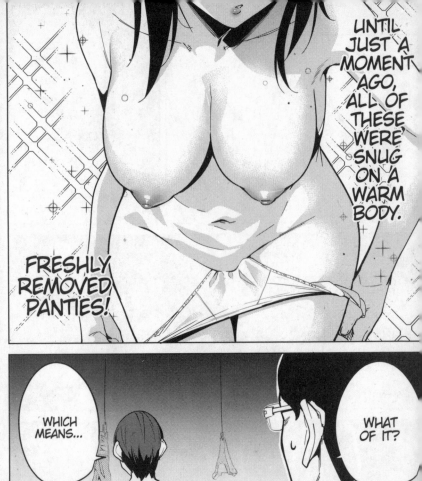

UNTIL JUST A MOMENT AGO, ALL OF THESE WERE SNUG ON A WARM BODY.

FRESHLY REMOVED PANTIES!

WHICH MEANS...

WHAT OF IT?

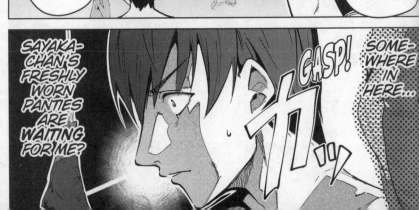

SAYAKA-CHAN'S FRESHLY WORN PANTIES ARE WAITING FOR ME?

GASP!

SOME- WHERE IN HERE...

WHICH ONES?!
FWSH
WHICH PAIR COULD BE HERS?
SHE'S SO INNOCENT. MAYBE SHE'D PREFER WHITE.
OR MAYBE COOL, SEXY BLACK ONES SINCE SHE'S THE WARDEN?

PER-HAPS...
KO... KOSUKE-KUN... ♡
SFF
DO-DON'T STARE AT ME...

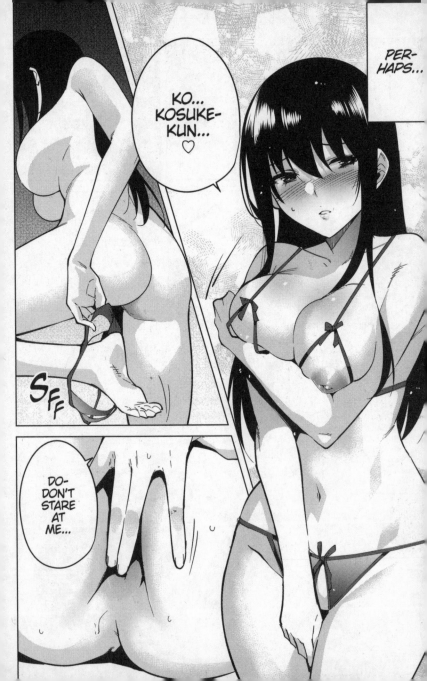

--KUN?
FUJI-SHIRO-KUN!!
SU... SUKE-KAWA-SAN.
WH-WHAT'S WRONG?
WHAT HAPPENED TO YOU, FUJI-SHIRO-KUN?
AS SOON AS YOU STARTED GOING AROUND SMELLING UNDER-WEAR...
YOU STARTED BABBLING A BUNCH OF NON-SENSE!
HUH ?!

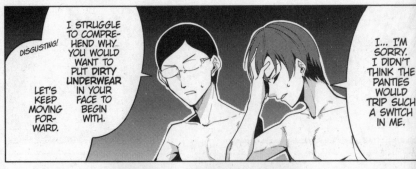

DISGUSTING!

I STRUGGLE TO COMPREHEND WHY YOU WOULD WANT TO PUT DIRTY UNDERWEAR IN YOUR FACE TO BEGIN WITH.

LET'S KEEP MOVING FORWARD.

I... I'M SORRY. I DIDN'T THINK THE PANTIES WOULD TRIP SUCH A SWITCH IN ME.

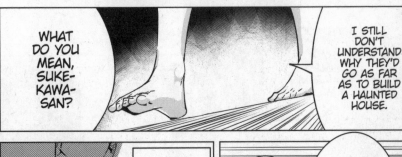

WHAT DO YOU MEAN, SUKEKAWA-SAN?

I STILL DON'T UNDERSTAND WHY THEY'D GO AS FAR AS TO BUILD A HAUNTED HOUSE.

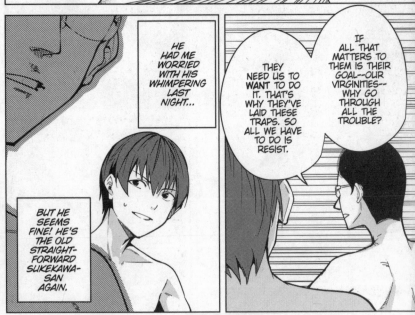

HE HAD ME WORRIED WITH HIS WHIMPERING LAST NIGHT...

BUT HE SEEMS FINE! HE'S THE OLD STRAIGHT-FORWARD SUKEKAWA-SAN AGAIN.

THEY NEED US TO WANT TO DO IT. THAT'S WHY THEY'VE LAID THESE TRAPS. SO ALL WE HAVE TO DO IS RESIST.

IF ALL THAT MATTERS TO THEM IS THEIR GOAL--OUR VIRGINITIES-- WHY GO THROUGH ALL THE TROUBLE?

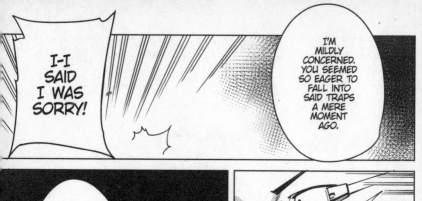

I-I SAID I WAS SORRY!

I'M MILDLY CONCERNED. YOU SEEMED SO EAGER TO FALL INTO SAID TRAPS A MERE MOMENT AGO.

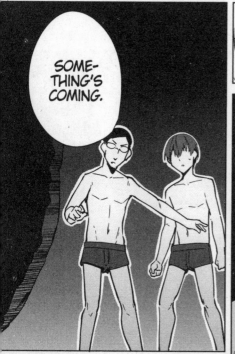

SOME-THING'S COMING.

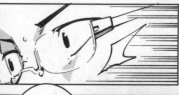

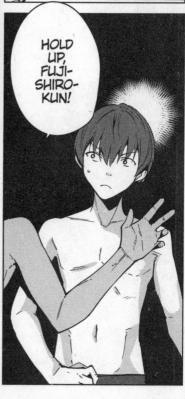

HOLD UP, FUJI-SHIRO-KUN!

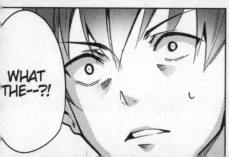

WHAT THE--?!

ZUMMM
ズ…
?!

WHAT... IS...?

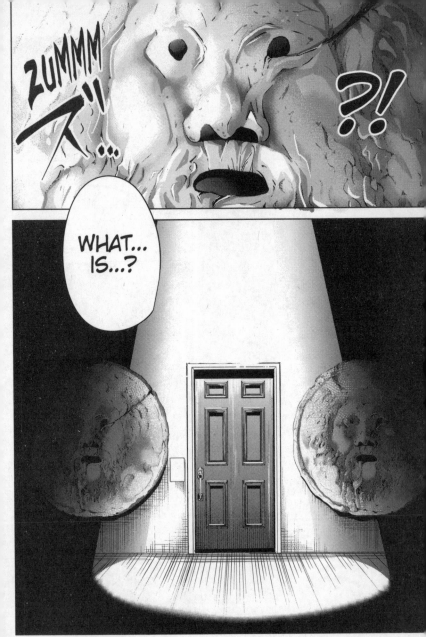

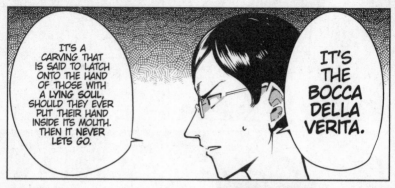

IT'S A CARVING THAT IS SAID TO LATCH ONTO THE HAND OF THOSE WITH A LYING SOUL, SHOULD THEY EVER PUT THEIR HAND INSIDE ITS MOUTH. THEN IT NEVER LETS GO.

IT'S THE BOCCA DELLA VERITA.

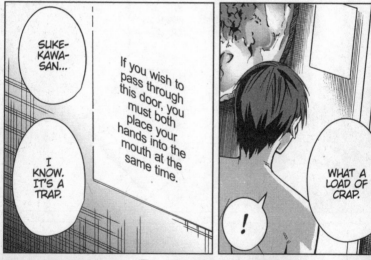

SUKE-KAWA-SAN...

If you wish to pass through this door, you must both place your hands into the mouth at the same time.

I KNOW. IT'S A TRAP.

!

WHAT A LOAD OF CRAP.

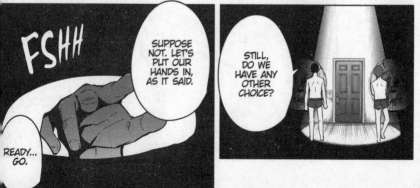

FSHH

SUPPOSE NOT. LET'S PUT OUR HANDS IN, AS IT SAID.

STILL, DO WE HAVE ANY OTHER CHOICE?

READY... GO.

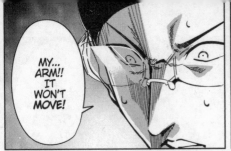

MY... ARM!! IT WON'T MOVE!

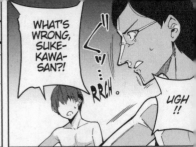

WHAT'S WRONG, SUKE-KAWA-SAN?!

RRCH.

UGH!!

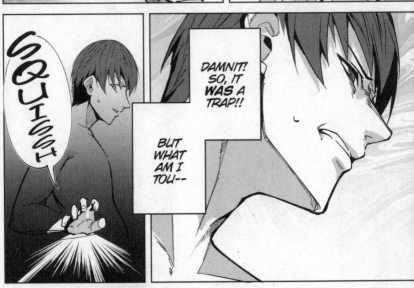

SQUICCH

DAMNIT! SO, IT WAS A TRAP!!

BUT WHAT AM I TOU--

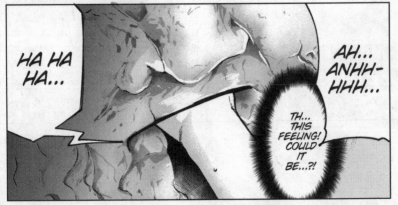

HA HA HA...

AH... ANHH-HHH...

TH... THIS FEELING! COULD IT BE...?!

SMIRK
YOU FELL FOR IT, DIPSHIT.
SQWSH
YOU KNOW WHAT THEY SAY, RIGHT? IF YOU'RE LYING, YOUR HAND IS MINE FOREVER.
YOU ACTUALLY WANT TO DO IT, BUT YOU'RE TRYING TO ACT LIKE A STRONG LITTLE VIRGIN. AREN'T YOU, LIAR?

DA-DUN
ONCE YOU DECIDE TO STOP LYING TO YOURSELF, PERHAPS YOU CAN GO FREE?
DA-DUN
WHAT SHOULD WE DO??

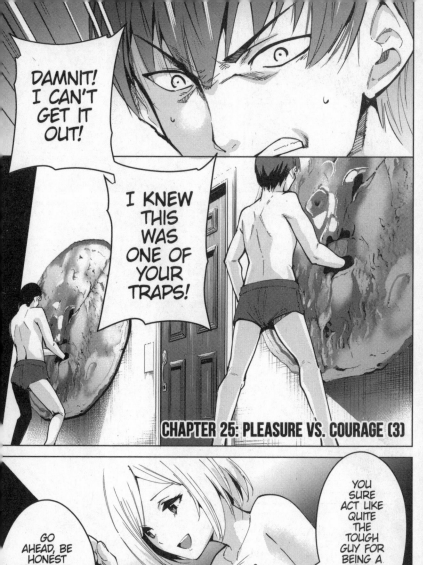

DAMNIT! I CAN'T GET IT OUT!

I KNEW THIS WAS ONE OF YOUR TRAPS!

CHAPTER 25: PLEASURE VS. COURAGE (3)

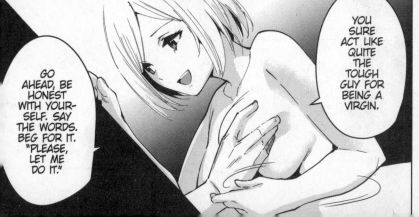

YOU SURE ACT LIKE QUITE THE TOUGH GUY FOR BEING A VIRGIN.

GO AHEAD, BE HONEST WITH YOURSELF. SAY THE WORDS. BEG FOR IT. "PLEASE, LET ME DO IT."

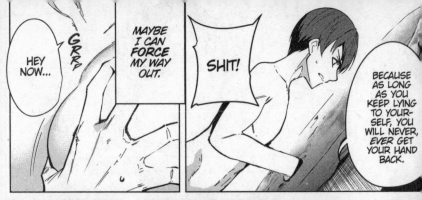

HEY NOW...

GRR

MAYBE I CAN FORCE MY WAY OUT.

SHIT!

BECAUSE AS LONG AS YOU KEEP LYING TO YOURSELF, YOU WILL NEVER, EVER GET YOUR HAND BACK.

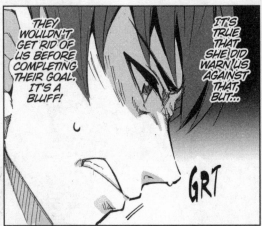

THEY WOULDN'T GET RID OF US BEFORE COMPLETING THEIR GOAL, IT'S A BLUFF!

IT'S TRUE THAT SHE DID WARN US AGAINST THAT, BUT...

GRT

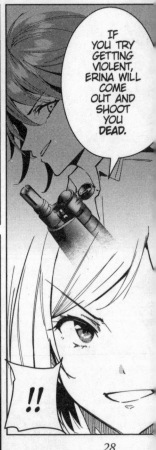

IF YOU TRY GETTING VIOLENT, ERINA WILL COME OUT AND SHOOT YOU DEAD.

!!

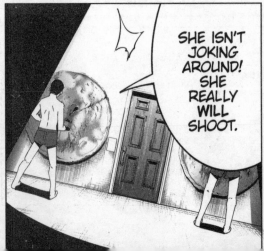

SHE ISN'T JOKING AROUND! SHE REALLY WILL SHOOT.

28

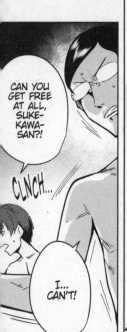

CAN YOU GET FREE AT ALL, SUKE-KAWA-SAN?!

CLNCH...

I.... CAN'T!

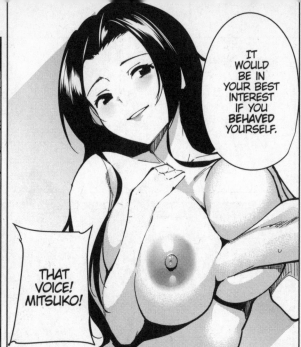

IT WOULD BE IN YOUR BEST INTEREST IF YOU BEHAVED YOURSELF.

THAT VOICE! MITSUKO!

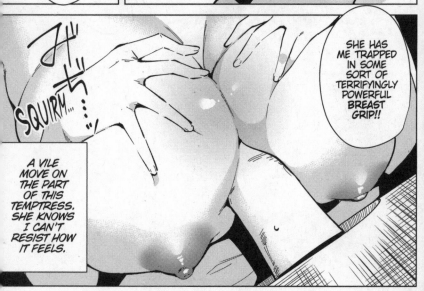

SHE HAS ME TRAPPED IN SOME SORT OF TERRIFYINGLY POWERFUL BREAST GRIP!!

SQUIRM...

A VILE MOVE ON THE PART OF THIS TEMPTRESS. SHE KNOWS I CAN'T RESIST HOW IT FEELS.

YOU'VE ALWAYS RESISTED WITH YOUR MOUTH...
BUT YOUR HAND IS DOING QUITE THE OPPO-SITE.
GWSH
......!!
AHHH... ♡
HOW COULD YOU... ♡
CAN YOU FEEL IT? MY NIPPLES ARE ALREADY HARD. ♡
JOLT
SHIT! MAYBE IF I LET MYSELF GET INTO IT, SHE WOULD LET ME GO!
GAH, I CAN'T FIGHT IT! IN MY HEAD I KNOW WHAT I HAVE TO DO, BUT MY HAND WON'T LISTEN!!
HAHH! ♡
DON'T YOU WANT TO HAVE A LITTLE MORE FUN?
WGGL
AHN! ♡

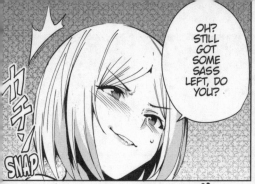

OH? STILL GOT SOME SASS LEFT, DO YOU?

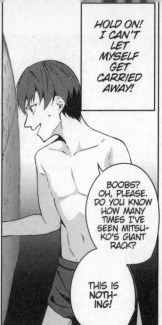

HOLD ON! I CAN'T LET MYSELF GET CARRIED AWAY!

BOOBS? OH, PLEASE. DO YOU KNOW HOW MANY TIMES I'VE SEEN MITSU-KO'S GIANT RACK?

THIS IS NOTHING!

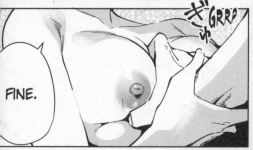

FINE.

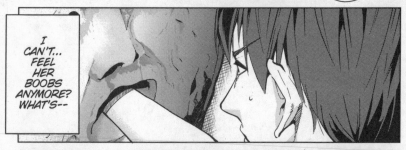

I CAN'T... FEEL HER BOOBS ANYMORE? WHAT'S--

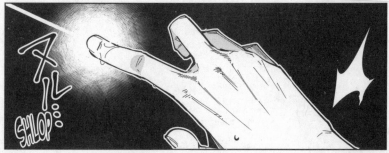

WH-
WHAT?!
JUST NOW... MY FINGER...
SLURP...
SHLURP...
COULD SHE BE... LICKING ME?!
SHLURRP
SHLIIP ♥
SHLOP
AHHN...♥
NN...
AHHN...♥
WH-WHAT IS THIS FEEL-ING?!

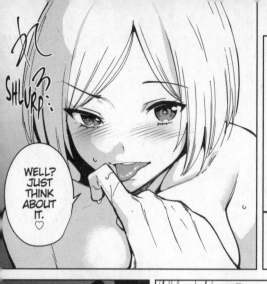

SHLURP?!

WELL? JUST THINK ABOUT IT. ♡

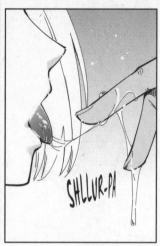

SHLLUR-PA

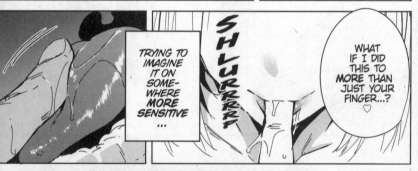

TRYING TO IMAGINE IT ON SOME-WHERE MORE SENSITIVE ...

SHLURRRP

WHAT IF I DID THIS TO MORE THAN JUST YOUR FINGER...? ♡

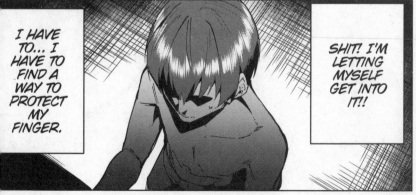

I HAVE TO... I HAVE TO FIND A WAY TO PROTECT MY FINGER.

SHIT! I'M LETTING MYSELF GET INTO IT!!

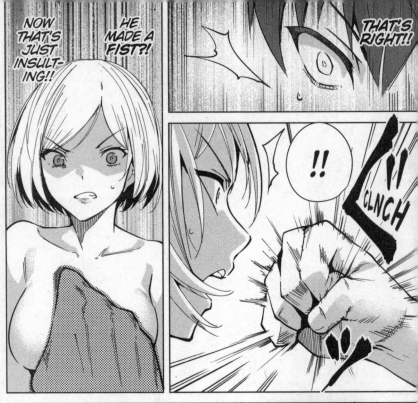

NOW THAT'S JUST INSULT-ING!!

HE MADE A FIST?!

THAT'S RIGHT!!

!!

CLNCH

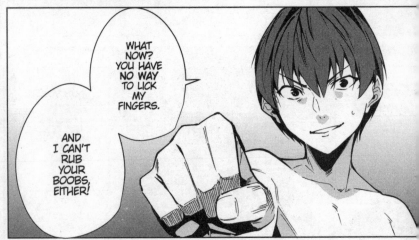

WHAT NOW? YOU HAVE NO WAY TO LICK MY FINGERS.

AND I CAN'T RUB YOUR BOOBS, EITHER!

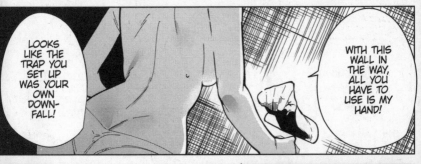

LOOKS LIKE THE TRAP YOU SET UP WAS YOUR OWN DOWNFALL!

WITH THIS WALL IN THE WAY, ALL YOU HAVE TO USE IS MY HAND!

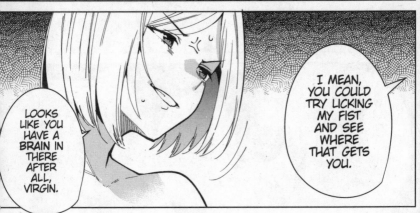

LOOKS LIKE YOU HAVE A BRAIN IN THERE AFTER ALL, VIRGIN.

I MEAN, YOU COULD TRY LICKING MY FIST AND SEE WHERE THAT GETS YOU.

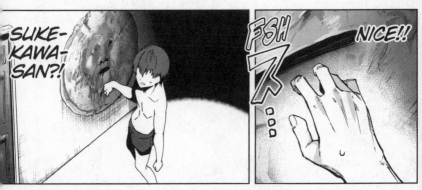

SUKE-KAWA-SAN?!

FSH

NICE!!

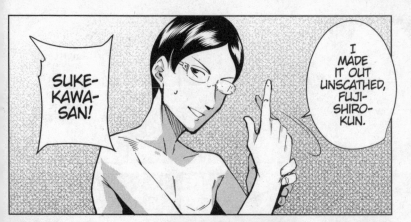

SUKE-KAWA-SAN!

I MADE IT OUT UNSCATHED, FUJI-SHIRO-KUN.

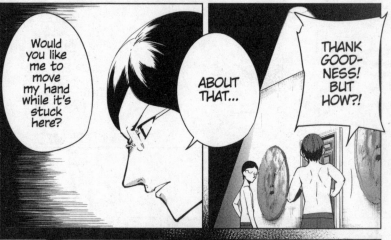

Would you like me to move my hand while it's stuck here?

ABOUT THAT...

THANK GOOD-NESS! BUT HOW?!

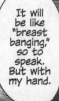

I have been interested in this form of play for a while, please let me experience it.

It will be like "breast banging," so to speak. But with my hand.

With breasts as enormous as yours, I do believe it will feel quite pleasurable.
Oh ho ho... ♡ You boys sure do like them, don't you?
I'm just happy you have finally faced your feelings. ♡
......
ZA
ZM
Now then... ♡

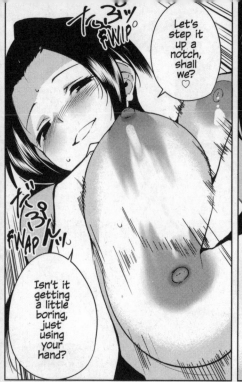

たぶッ
FWIP

Let's step it up a notch, shall we? ♡

だ。ぶッ
FWAP ベリ

Isn't it getting a little boring, just using your hand?

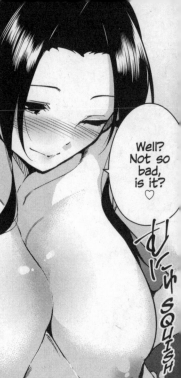

Well? Not so bad, is it? ♡

むにゅぶにゅ
SQUISH

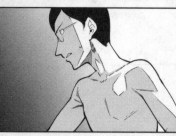

Even a germaphobe like me would have trouble refusing this technique! But...

This perfect amount of pressure! And the unbelievable softness! If it wasn't my hand, but the actual thing...

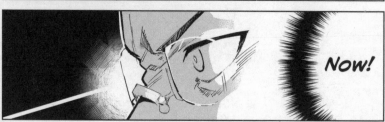

Now!

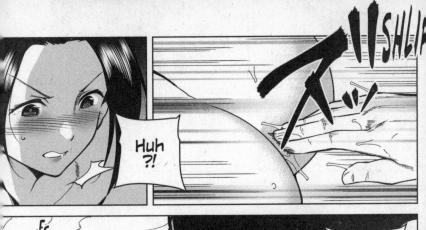

SHLIP

HUH ?!

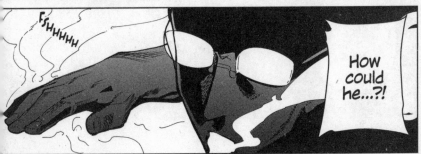

FSHHHHH

HOW COULD HE...?!

ALL I HAD TO DO WAS WAIT FOR HER TO WORK UP A SWEAT.

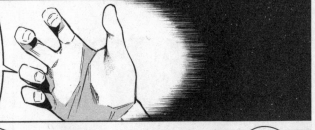

IT'S A LITTLE EARLY TO BE PATTING YOURSELVES ON THE BACK!

!!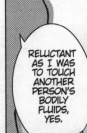

RELUCTANT AS I WAS TO TOUCH ANOTHER PERSON'S BODILY FLUIDS, YES.

NO WAY! YOU USED HER SWEAT TO SLIDE YOUR HAND OUT!

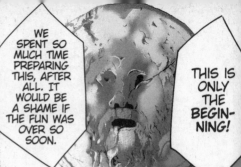

PLEASE, ENJOY YOURSELVES.

WE SPENT SO MUCH TIME PREPARING THIS, AFTER ALL. IT WOULD BE A SHAME IF THE FUN WAS OVER SO SOON.

THIS IS ONLY THE BEGINNING!

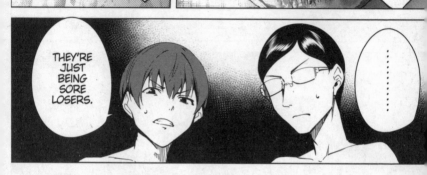

THEY'RE JUST BEING SORE LOSERS.

....

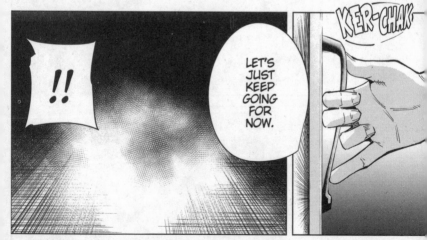

!!

LET'S JUST KEEP GOING FOR NOW.

KER-CHAK

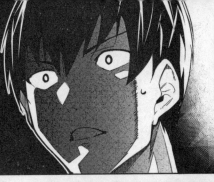

IT'S SO DARK! COMPLETELY PITCH BLACK!

YOU MEAN WE HAVE TO FIND OUR WAY OUT COMPLETELY BLIND?!

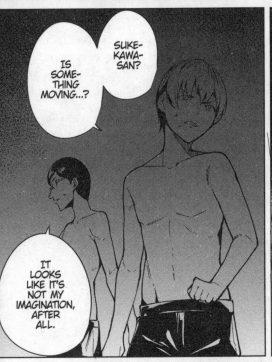

IS SOMETHING MOVING...?

SUKE-KAWA-SAN?

IT LOOKS LIKE IT'S NOT MY IMAGINATION, AFTER ALL.

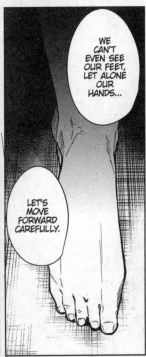

WE CAN'T EVEN SEE OUR FEET, LET ALONE OUR HANDS...

LET'S MOVE FORWARD CAREFULLY.

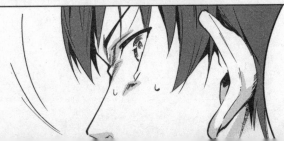

SOMEONE'S HERE...

?!
DA-DUN
FUCK, BEHIND YOU!!

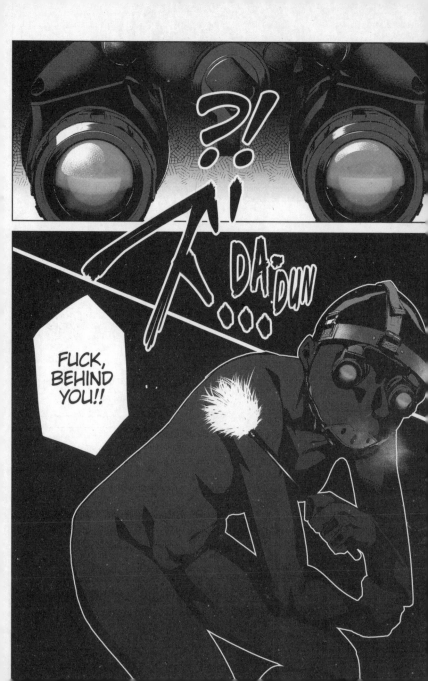

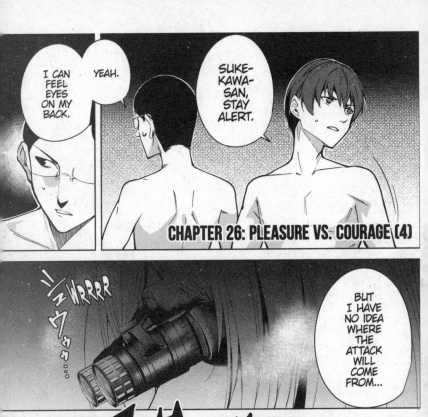

I CAN FEEL EYES ON MY BACK.

YEAH.

SUKEKAWA-SAN, STAY ALERT.

CHAPTER 26: PLEASURE VS. COURAGE (4)

WRRRR

BUT I HAVE NO IDEA WHERE THE ATTACK WILL COME FROM...

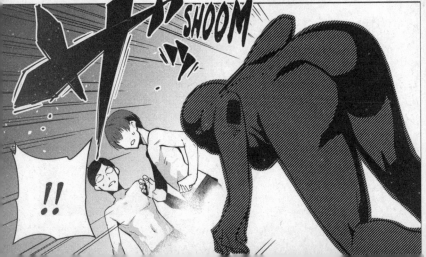

SHOOM

!!

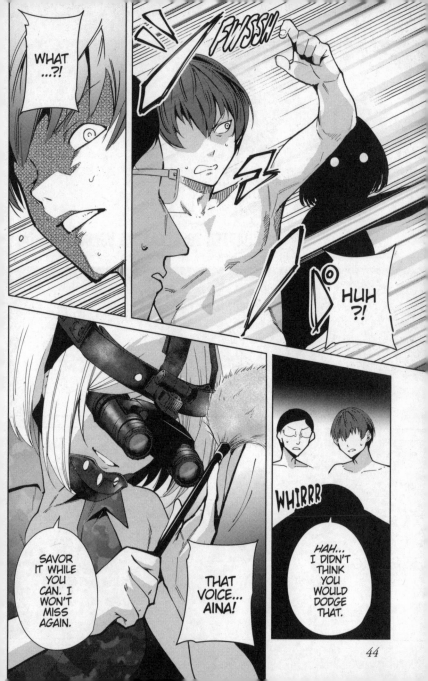

WHAT...?!

FWSSH

HUH ?!

SAVOR IT WHILE YOU CAN. I WON'T MISS AGAIN.

THAT VOICE... AINA!

WHIRRR

HAH... I DIDN'T THINK YOU WOULD DODGE THAT.

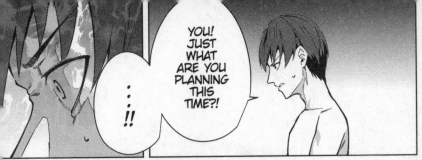

YOU! JUST WHAT ARE YOU PLANNING THIS TIME?!

...!!

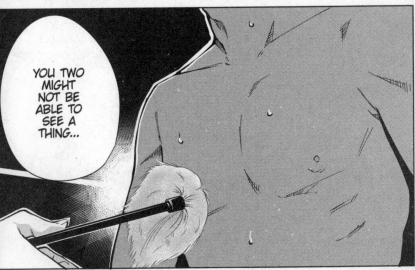

YOU TWO MIGHT NOT BE ABLE TO SEE A THING...

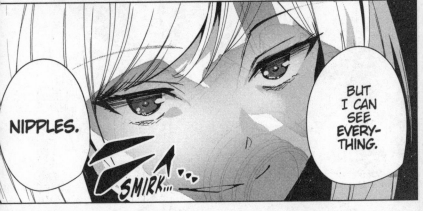

BUT I CAN SEE EVERYTHING.

NIPPLES.

SMIRK...

45

SHAAA
スリ…
HEY! ST--
SHA
スリ
THIS IS CALLED THE "TICKLER." AND IT'S JUST LIKE IT SAYS ON THE TIN.
IN S&M PLAY, A PERSON WILL USE IT ON THEIR BLIND-FOLDED PARTNER.
DID YOU KNOW WITH HUMANS, IF YOU SMOTHER ONE OF THEIR FIVE SENSES...
THE OTHER FOUR BECOME EVEN SHARPER, MAKING UP FOR THE ONE THEY CAN'T USE?
FOR EXAMPLE, BY ROBBING YOU OF YOUR SIGHT...
FWIP
I'M INCREAS-ING THE POWER OF YOUR SENSE OF TOUCH.
FEELING SENSI-TIVE?

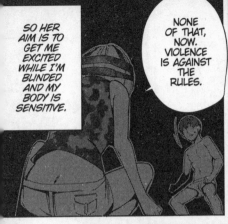

SO HER AIM IS TO GET ME EXCITED WHILE I'M BLINDED AND MY BODY IS SENSITIVE.

NONE OF THAT, NOW. VIOLENCE IS AGAINST THE RULES.

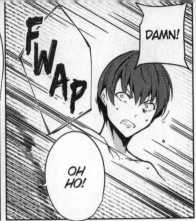

FWAP

DAMN!

OH HO!

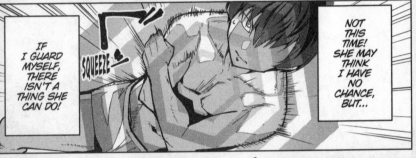

IF I GUARD MYSELF, THERE ISN'T A THING SHE CAN DO!

SQUEEZE

NOT THIS TIME! SHE MAY THINK I HAVE NO CHANCE, BUT...

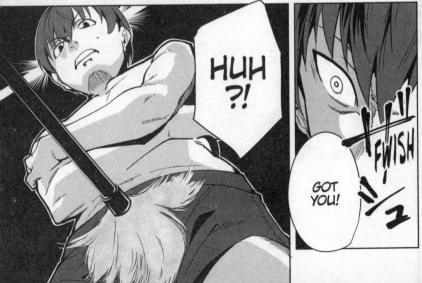

HUH ?!

FWISH

GOT YOU!

HEE HEE... ♡ DID YOU THINK YOUR NIPPLES WERE YOUR ONLY WEAK SPOT?
DAMN, RIGHT IN MY ACHILLES BULGE!
CLNCH
SEE? NOW YOUR NIPPLES ARE WIDE OPEN. ♡
AGH!
FWIP
DAMNIT! THIS ISN'T GOOD.
HAHH
IF I COVER UP MY NIPPLES, MY PRIVATES ARE WIDE OPEN, AND COVERING DOWN THERE JUST LEAVES MY NIPPLES OPEN!
HAHH
AND OVER HERE, TOO.
AH!
JOLT

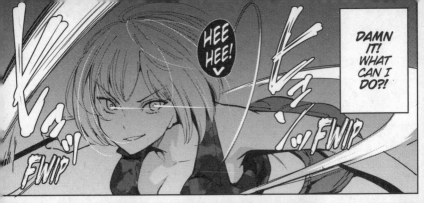

HEE HEE! ♥

DAMN IT! WHAT CAN I DO?!

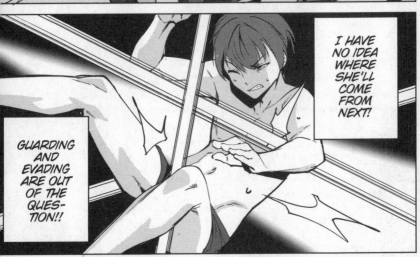

I HAVE NO IDEA WHERE SHE'LL COME FROM NEXT!

GUARDING AND EVADING ARE OUT OF THE QUESTION!!

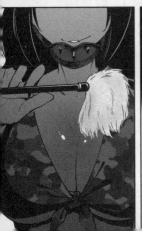

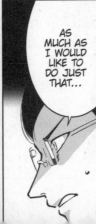

AS MUCH AS I WOULD LIKE TO DO JUST THAT...

SORRY, FUJI-SHIRO-KUN.

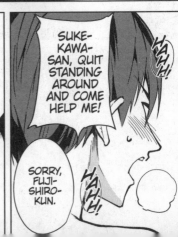

SUKE-KAWA-SAN, QUIT STANDING AROUND AND COME HELP ME!

HAHH!

HAHH!

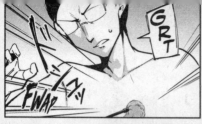

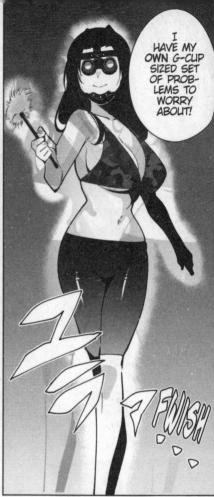

I HAVE MY OWN G-CUP SIZED SET OF PROBLEMS TO WORRY ABOUT!

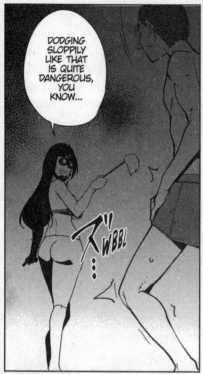

DODGING SLOPPILY LIKE THAT IS QUITE DANGEROUS, YOU KNOW...

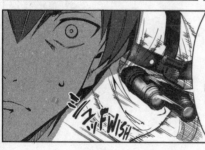

SHOULD YOU REALLY BE LOOKING OVER THERE?

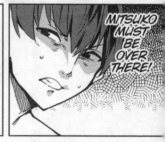

MITSUKO MUST BE OVER THERE!

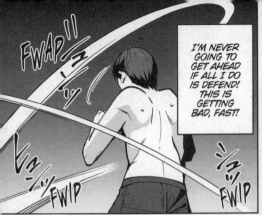

FWAP!!

FWIP

FWIP

I'M NEVER GOING TO GET AHEAD IF ALL I DO IS DEFEND! THIS IS GETTING BAD, FAST!

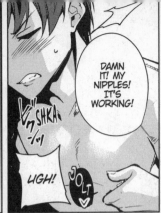

VMSHKA

UGH!

JOLT

DAMN IT! MY NIPPLES! IT'S WORKING!

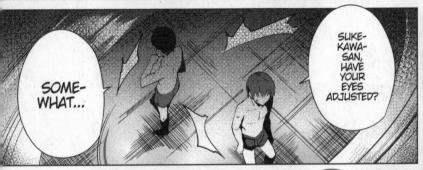

SOME-WHAT...

SUKE-KAWA-SAN, HAVE YOUR EYES ADJUSTED?

IF WE CAN'T GUARD OR EVADE, THEN OUR ONLY OPTION IS...

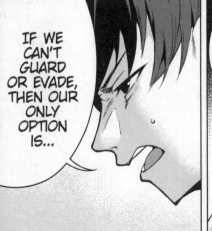

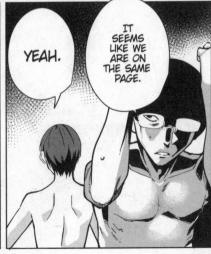

YEAH.

IT SEEMS LIKE WE ARE ON THE SAME PAGE.

FWOOOM
CHAAAAARGE!!
WHA--?!
HAHH!
HAHH!
DID WE GET AWAY?
I THINK SO.
GAHHH, SERIOUSLY?! AFTER ALL THAT, I GET A BONER FROM ESCAPING?!

BUT HOW DO WE...
IT SEEMS WE WILL NEED TO CHOOSE SEPARATE ROUTES.
From this point on, all guests must choose a single door each.
THIS IS ALSO OBVIOUSLY A TRAP...
point on, all guests must choose a single door
NO TIME TO DROP OUR GUARD NOW!
ARE YOU GOOD WITH THAT DOOR?
YES, THEIR RULES ARE CLEAR.
GRP
KRIIIIK
HUNH. I SHOULD HAVE GUESSED...

?!
DO YOUR BEST TO MAKE YOUR SCREAMS NICE AND CUTE.
YOU WON'T LET ME DOWN, WILL YOU?
SHLURP...

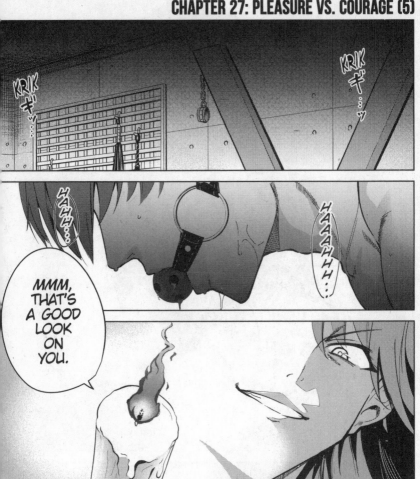

KRIK ギ…ッ

KRIK ギ…ッ

HAAH…

HAAAHHH…

MMM, THAT'S A GOOD LOOK ON YOU.

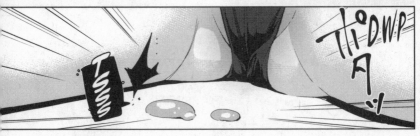

TSSS

FDWP

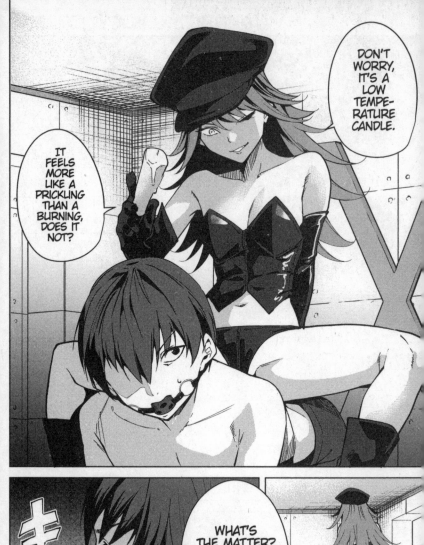

DON'T WORRY, IT'S A LOW TEMPE-RATURE CANDLE.

IT FEELS MORE LIKE A PRICKLING THAN A BURNING, DOES IT NOT?

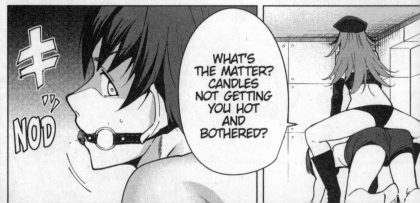

WHAT'S THE MATTER? CANDLES NOT GETTING YOU HOT AND BOTHERED?

NOD

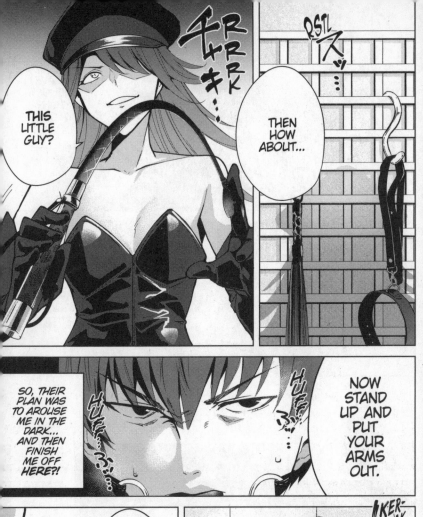

THIS LITTLE GUY?

THEN HOW ABOUT...

ЯSTL

SO, THEIR PLAN WAS TO AROUSE ME IN THE DARK... AND THEN FINISH ME OFF HERE?!

NOW STAND UP AND PUT YOUR ARMS OUT.

HUFF...?

HUFF...?

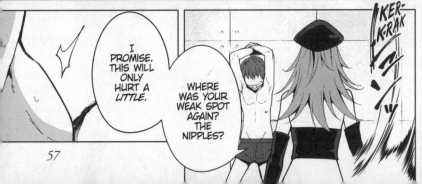

I PROMISE. THIS WILL ONLY HURT A *LITTLE*.

WHERE WAS YOUR WEAK SPOT AGAIN? THE NIPPLES?

KER-KRAK

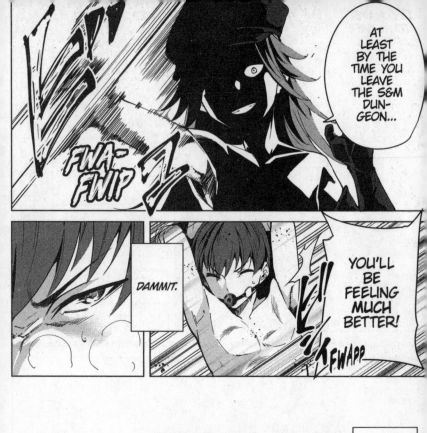

AT LEAST BY THE TIME YOU LEAVE THE S&M DUNGEON...

FWA- FWIP

DAMMIT.

YOU'LL BE FEELING MUCH BETTER!

FWAPP

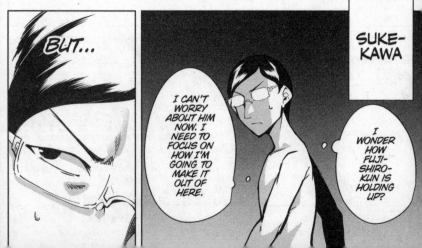

BUT...

SUKE- KAWA

I CAN'T WORRY ABOUT HIM NOW. I NEED TO FOCUS ON HOW I'M GOING TO MAKE IT OUT OF HERE.

I WONDER HOW FUJI- SHIRO-KUN IS HOLDING UP?

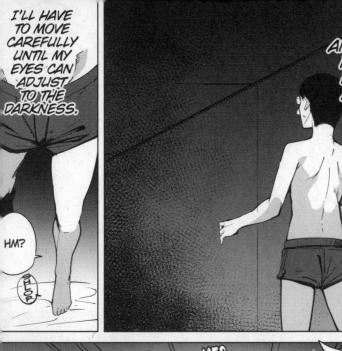

I'LL HAVE TO MOVE CAREFULLY UNTIL MY EYES CAN ADJUST TO THE DARKNESS.

IT'S ANOTHER PITCH-BLACK AREA.

HM?

SHLOP

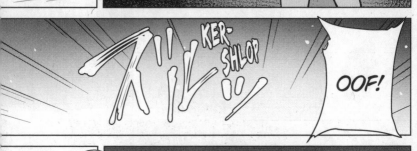

KER-SHLOP

OOF!

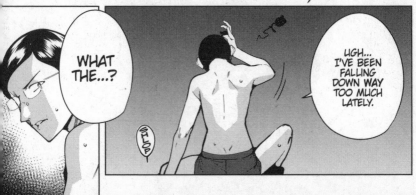

WHAT THE...?

SHLOP

UGH... I'VE BEEN FALLING DOWN WAY TOO MUCH LATELY.

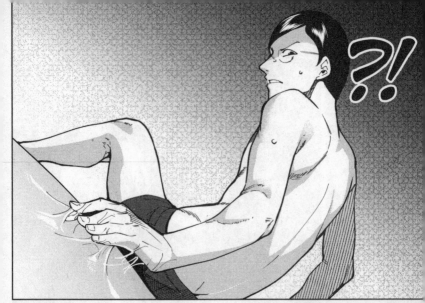

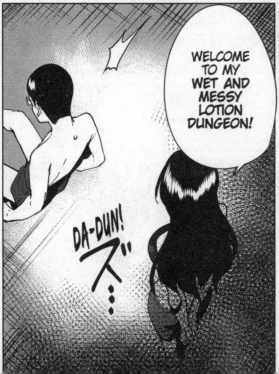

WELCOME TO MY WET AND MESSY LOTION DUNGEON!

DA-DUN!

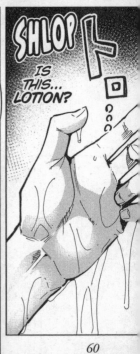

SHLOP

IS THIS... LOTION?

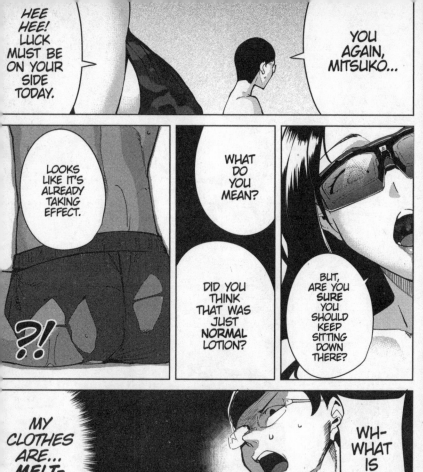

HEE HEE! LUCK MUST BE ON YOUR SIDE TODAY.

YOU AGAIN, MITSUKO...

LOOKS LIKE IT'S ALREADY TAKING EFFECT.

?!

WHAT DO YOU MEAN?

DID YOU THINK THAT WAS JUST NORMAL LOTION?

BUT, ARE YOU SURE YOU SHOULD KEEP SITTING DOWN THERE?

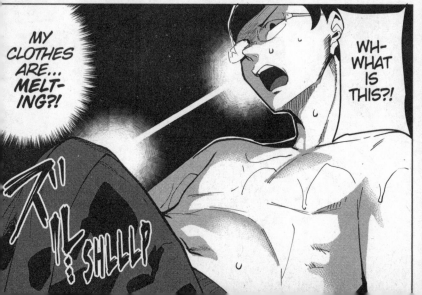

MY CLOTHES ARE... MELTING?!

WH-WHAT IS THIS?!

SHLLLP

THAT'S RIGHT! THIS LOTION WAS SPECIALLY CREATED TO BREAK DOWN FABRICS.
OF COURSE, IT WON'T CAUSE ANY HARM TO YOUR BODY.
DAMN ...!
SHLAP
OOH, I WOULDN'T TRY RUNNING AWAY IF I WERE YOU.
UGH!
SHLIPP
DAMN!
YOU'LL JUST FALL AND GET EVEN MORE OILED UP! AND WOULDN'T YOU JUST HATE THAT?

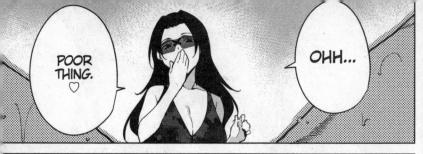

POOR THING. ♡

OHH...

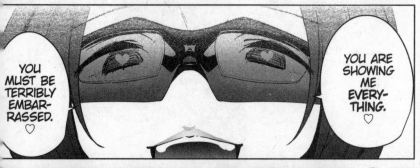

YOU MUST BE TERRIBLY EMBARRASSED. ♡

YOU ARE SHOWING ME EVERYTHING. ♡

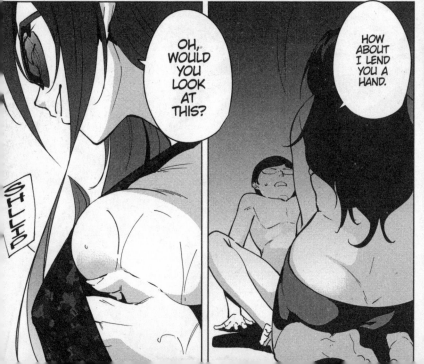

OH, WOULD YOU LOOK AT THIS?

HOW ABOUT I LEND YOU A HAND.

SHLLIP

I SEEM TO HAVE GOTTEN A SMUDGE OF LOTION ON MY CLOTHES AS WELL!
SHAAA
SHRRRP
ドロ...
EVERY-THING I WAS WEARING IS JUST MELTING AWAY...♡

IF WE ARE ALL COVERED IN LOTION LIKE THIS, WE CAN'T CONTROL OURSELVES...
BWOMM
SO, YOU'LL HAVE TO FORGIVE ME IF SOMETHING JUST MIRACULOUSLY... HAPPENS.
LIKE, IF YOU WERE TO TRY TO ESCAPE, YOU COULD SLIP...
YOU COULD SLIP RIGHT INTO ME, OR ON TOP OF ME, OR... *INTO* ME.
IT'S NOT YOUR FAULT, THOUGH. IT WOULD BE AN ACCIDENT, RIGHT?

03

DESTINY LOVERS

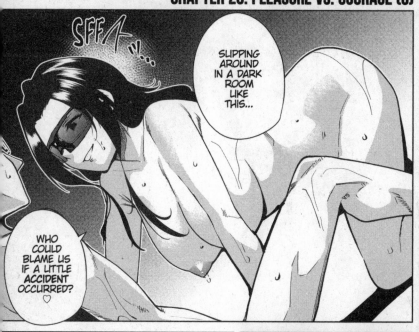

SFFA...

SLIPPING AROUND IN A DARK ROOM LIKE THIS...

WHO COULD BLAME US IF A LITTLE ACCIDENT OCCURRED? ♡

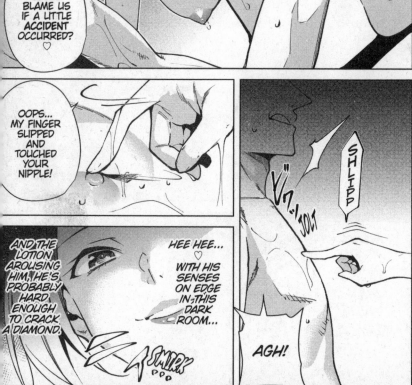

OOPS... MY FINGER SLIPPED AND TOUCHED YOUR NIPPLE!

SHLIPP

JOLT

AND THE LOTION AROUSING HIM, HE'S PROBABLY HARD ENOUGH TO CRACK A DIAMOND.

SMIRK

HEE HEE... ♡ WITH HIS SENSES ON EDGE IN THIS DARK ROOM...

AGH!

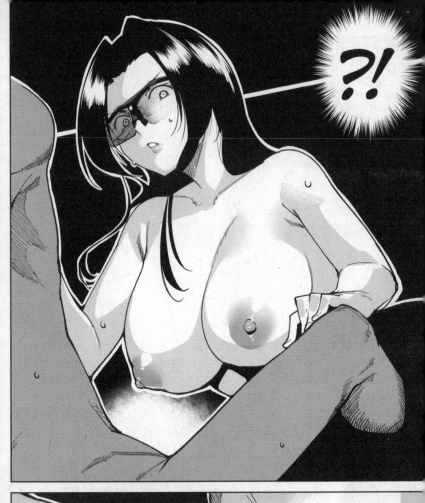

?!

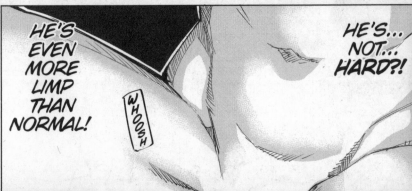

HE'S
EVEN
MORE
LIMP
THAN
NORMAL!

WHOOSH

HE'S...
NOT...
HARD?!

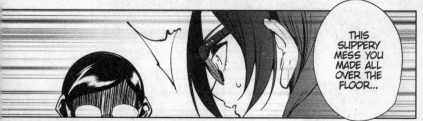

THIS SLIPPERY MESS YOU MADE ALL OVER THE FLOOR...

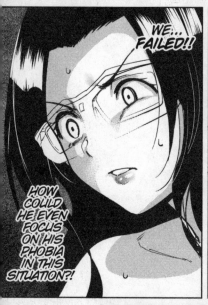

WE... FAILED!!

HOW COULD HE EVEN FOCUS ON HIS PHOBIA IN THIS SITUATION?!

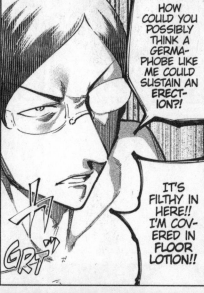

HOW COULD YOU POSSIBLY THINK A GERMA-PHOBE LIKE ME COULD SUSTAIN AN ERECT-ION?!

IT'S FILTHY IN HERE!! I'M COV-ERED IN FLOOR LOTION!!

GRT

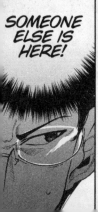

SOMEONE ELSE IS HERE!

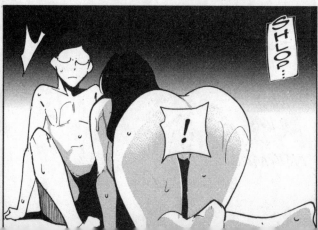

SHLOP...

!

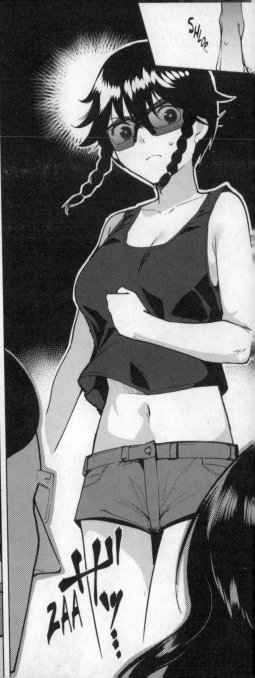

SHLOP...

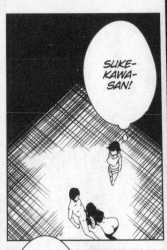

SUKE-KAWA-SAN!

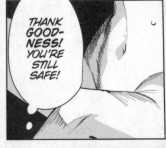

THANK GOOD-NESS! YOU'RE STILL SAFE!

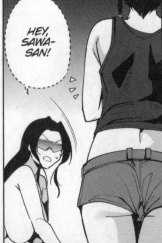

HEY, SAWA-SAN!

ZAA

DO SOMETHING ABOUT THIS USELESS BOY!
CLNCH
HUH? WAIT... MITSUKO-SAN!
AH!
SHLIP
KER-SHLUMP
AHHHH!
WHAT ARE YOU DOING?!
DAMNIT... SOMEONE ELSE? BUT WHO?
THIS SCENT ...
SNFF

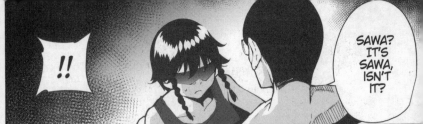

SAWA? IT'S SAWA, ISN'T IT?

!!

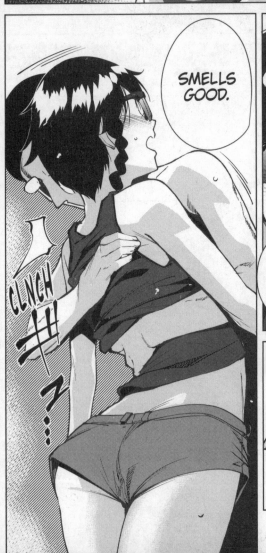

SMELLS GOOD.

CLNCH !!

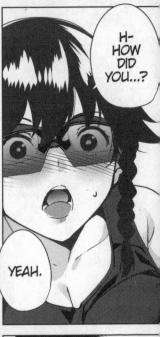

H-HOW DID YOU...?

YEAH.

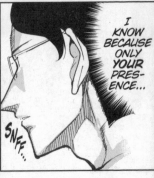

I KNOW BECAUSE ONLY YOUR PRES-ENCE...

SNFF...

72

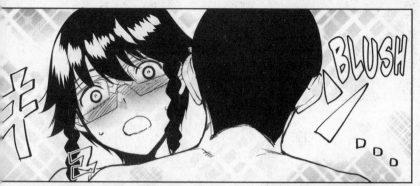

BLUSH

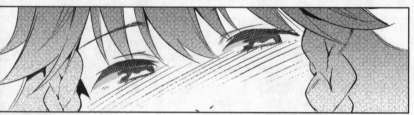

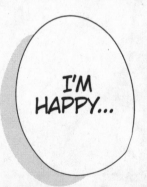

I'M HAPPY...

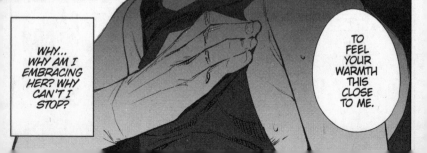

WHY... WHY AM I EMBRACING HER? WHY CAN'T I STOP?

TO FEEL YOUR WARMTH THIS CLOSE TO ME.

I... I FEEL SO AT PEACE LIKE THIS...
WHAT... IS THIS FEEL-ING...?
I CAN FEEL MY BODY GETTING WARMER AND WARMER...
SQUEEZE
WHY OOO?
BA-DUM

SHF

AHN...
OHM...
HAHH...
HAHH...
HAHH...
HAHH...
SUKE-KAWA-SAN...
HAHH...
GRRRM
WOW...

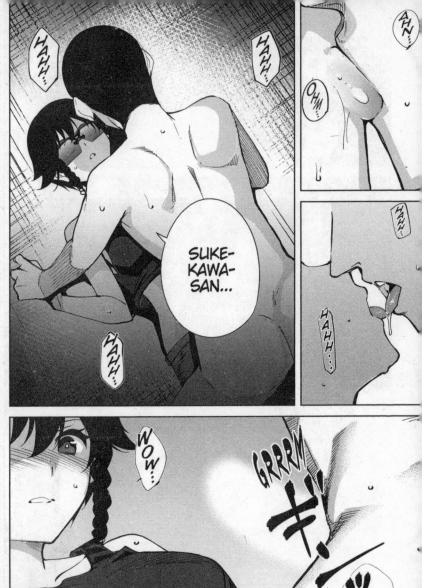

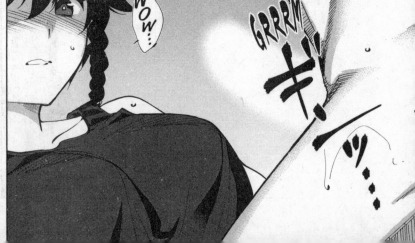

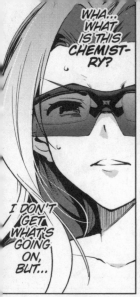

WHA... WHAT IS THIS CHEMISTRY?

I DON'T GET WHAT'S GOING ON, BUT...

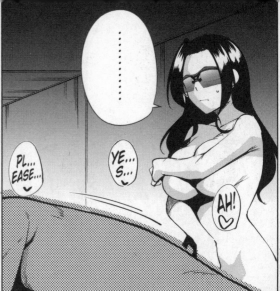

....

PL... EASE...

YE... S...

AH! ♡

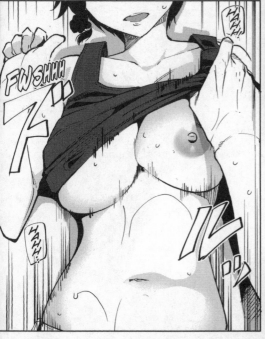

FWSHHH

HAHH!

HAHH!

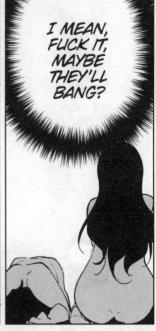

I MEAN, FUCK IT, MAYBE THEY'LL BANG?

I... I...
YOU...

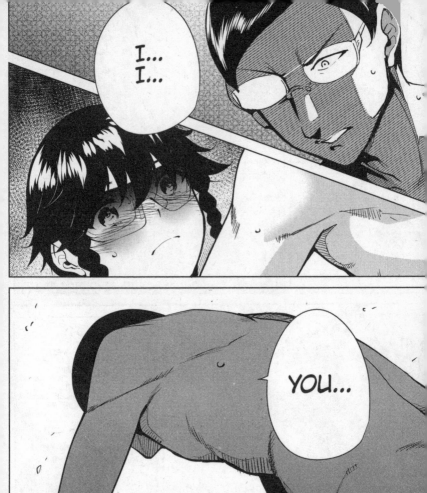

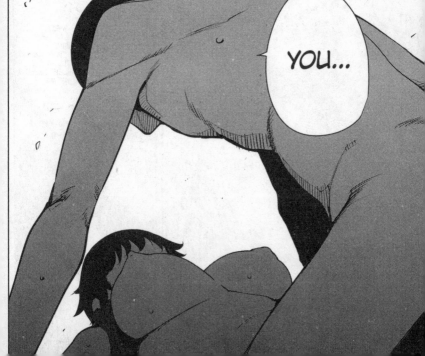

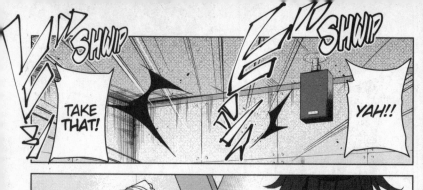

TAKE THAT!

YAH!!

HAH...

HAH

CHAPTER 29: PLEASURE VS. COURAGE (7)

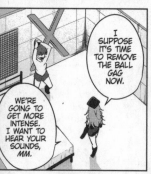

I SUPPOSE IT'S TIME TO REMOVE THE BALL GAG NOW.

WE'RE GOING TO GET MORE INTENSE. I WANT TO HEAR YOUR SOUNDS, MM.

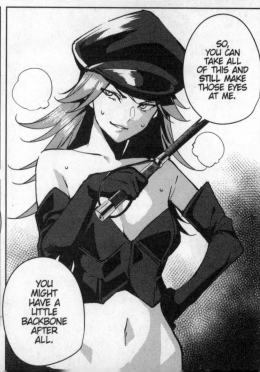

SO, YOU CAN TAKE ALL OF THIS AND STILL MAKE THOSE EYES AT ME.

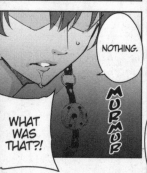

NOTHING.

WHAT WAS THAT?!

MURMUR

YOU MIGHT HAVE A LITTLE BACKBONE AFTER ALL.

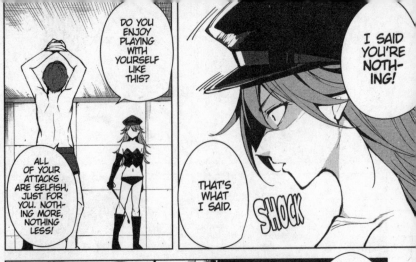

DO YOU ENJOY PLAYING WITH YOURSELF LIKE THIS?

ALL OF YOUR ATTACKS ARE SELFISH, JUST FOR YOU. NOTHING MORE, NOTHING LESS!

I SAID YOU'RE NOTHING!

THAT'S WHAT I SAID.

SHOCK

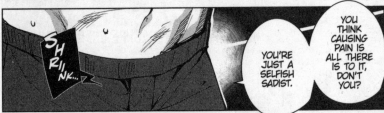

SHRIINK...

YOU THINK CAUSING PAIN IS ALL THERE IS TO IT, DON'T YOU?

YOU'RE JUST A SELFISH SADIST.

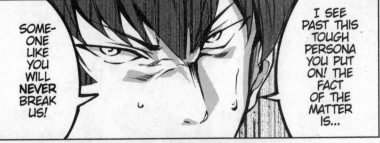

SOMEONE LIKE YOU WILL NEVER BREAK US!

I SEE PAST THIS TOUGH PERSONA YOU PUT ON! THE FACT OF THE MATTER IS...

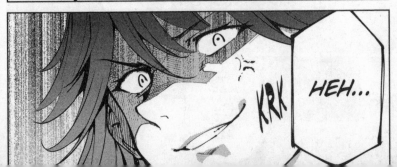

KRK

HEH...

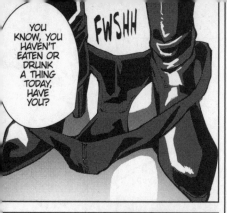

YOU KNOW, YOU HAVEN'T EATEN OR DRUNK A THING TODAY, HAVE YOU?

FWSHH

LOOKS LIKE I MADE A MISTAKE.

FWOP

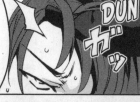

YOU'RE PROBABLY IRRITATED BECAUSE YOU'RE SO THIRSTY.

DUN

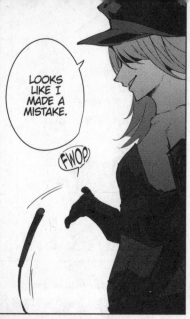

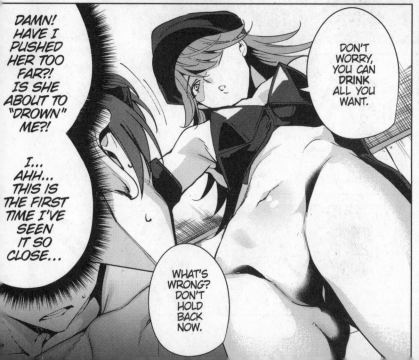

DAMN! HAVE I PUSHED HER TOO FAR?! IS SHE ABOUT TO "DROWN" ME?!

I... AHH... THIS IS THE FIRST TIME I'VE SEEN IT SO CLOSE...

DON'T WORRY, YOU CAN DRINK ALL YOU WANT.

WHAT'S WRONG? DON'T HOLD BACK NOW.

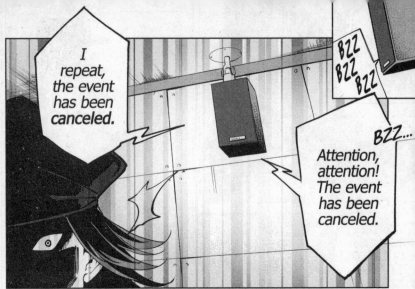

BZZ
BZZ
BZZ

I repeat, the event has been canceled.

BZZ...

Attention, attention! The event has been canceled.

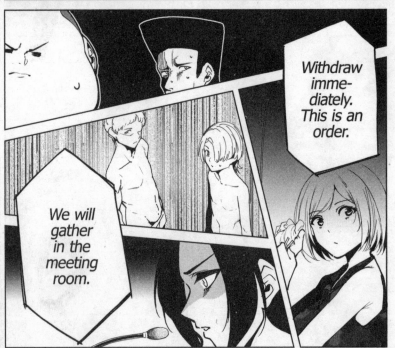

Withdraw immediately. This is an order.

We will gather in the meeting room.

82

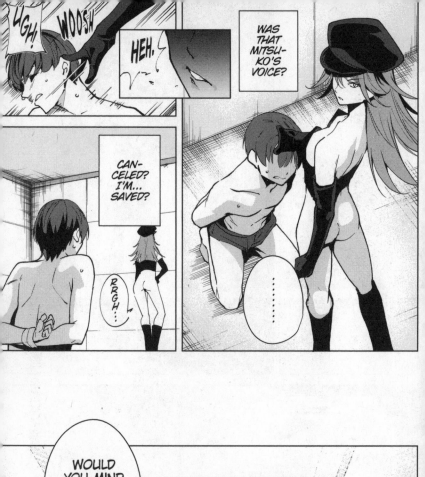

UGH! WOOSH!

HEH,

WAS THAT MITSU-KO'S VOICE?

CAN-CELED? I'M... SAVED?

RRGH...

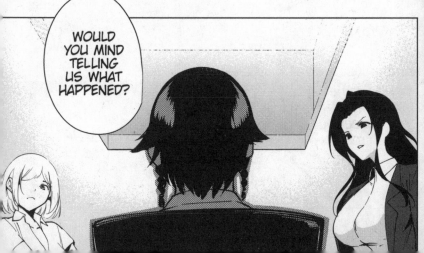

WOULD YOU MIND TELLING US WHAT HAPPENED?

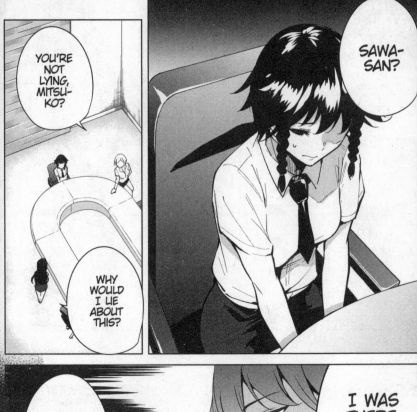

YOU'RE NOT LYING, MITSU-KO?

SAWA-SAN?

WHY WOULD I LIE ABOUT THIS?

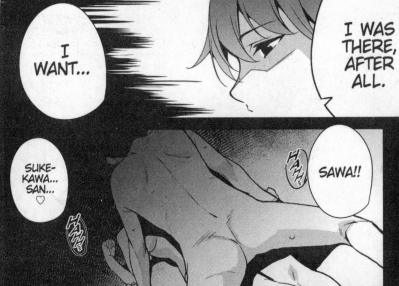

I WANT...

I WAS THERE, AFTER ALL.

SUKE-KAWA... SAN... ♡

HAH!

SAWA!!

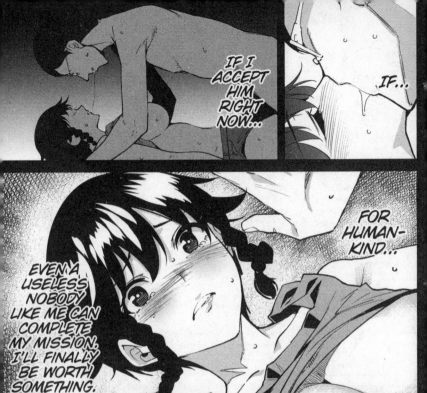

IF I ACCEPT HIM RIGHT NOW...

IF...

FOR HUMAN-KIND...

EVEN A USELESS NOBODY LIKE ME CAN COMPLETE MY MISSION, I'LL FINALLY BE WORTH SOMETHING.

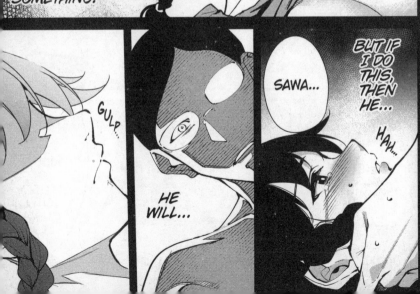

BUT IF I DO THIS, THEN HE...

SAWA...

HAH...

GULP...

HE WILL...

FWAK
I CAN'T!
WAI--
SAWA-SAN!
TMP
SHE REFUSED AND RAN AWAY, RIGHT AS HE WAS ABOUT TO...
CLNCH
ARE YOU KIDDING ME?? ABSO-LUTELY USE-LESS!
WHEN WILL WE GET ANOTHER GOLDEN OPPORTUNITY LIKE THAT?!

C'MON, BOSS, WE CAN'T KEEP HER AROUND AFTER A SCREW-UP LIKE THAT!
SAWA... DO YOU HAVE ANYTHING TO SAY FOR YOURSELF?
......
I SEE.
THIS WAS YOUR FAILURE, BUT IT AFFECTS US AS A WHOLE.
I'M SORRY, BUT...

WE WILL BE REMOVING YOU FROM THE TEAM.
!!
YOU WILL BE TRANS-FERRED.
IF I'M GOING TO BE TRANS-FERRED...
I'LL NEVER BE ABLE TO SEE SUKE-KAWA-SAN AGAIN!

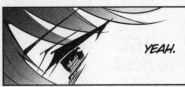

IF WE CONTINUE LIKE THIS... THEN I WILL END UP...

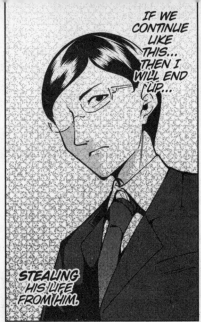

STEALING HIS LIFE FROM HIM.

YEAH.

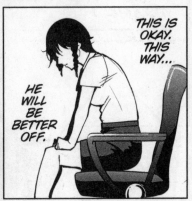

THIS IS OKAY. THIS WAY...

HE WILL BE BETTER OFF.

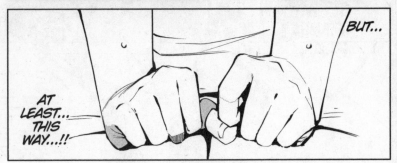

BUT...

AT LEAST... THIS WAY...!!

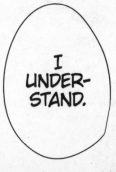

I UNDERSTAND.

OF COURSE, I WILL ACCEPT THE TRANSFER.
BUT I HAVE ONE REQUEST.
BEFORE YOU ALL SEE ME OFF, I HAVE AN IDEA!
I WANT YOU TO LISTEN TO MY FINAL PLAN!

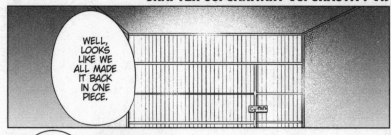

WELL, LOOKS LIKE WE ALL MADE IT BACK IN ONE PIECE.

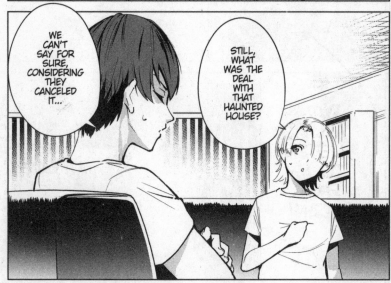

WE CAN'T SAY FOR SURE, CONSIDERING THEY CANCELED IT...

STILL, WHAT WAS THE DEAL WITH THAT HAUNTED HOUSE?

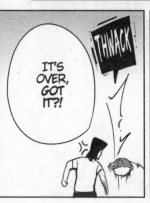

IT'S OVER, GOT IT?!

THWACK

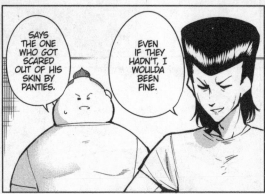

SAYS THE ONE WHO GOT SCARED OUT OF HIS SKIN BY PANTIES.

EVEN IF THEY HADN'T, I WOULDA BEEN FINE.

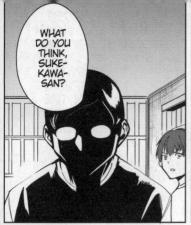

WHAT DO YOU THINK, SUKE-KAWA-SAN?

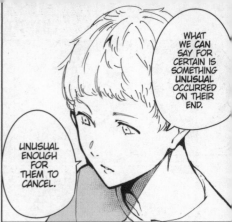

WHAT WE CAN SAY FOR CERTAIN IS SOMETHING UNUSUAL OCCURRED ON THEIR END.

UNUSUAL ENOUGH FOR THEM TO CANCEL.

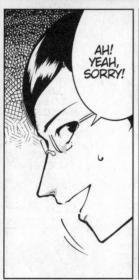

AH! YEAH, SORRY!

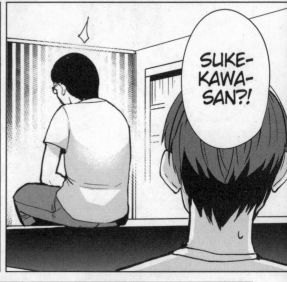

SUKE-KAWA-SAN?!

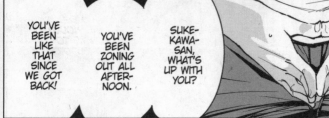

YOU'VE BEEN LIKE THAT SINCE WE GOT BACK!

YOU'VE BEEN ZONING OUT ALL AFTER-NOON.

SUKE-KAWA-SAN, WHAT'S UP WITH YOU?

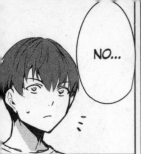

NO...

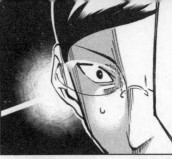

DOES IT HAVE ANYTHING TO DO WITH WHAT HAPPENED IN THE HAUNTED HOUSE?

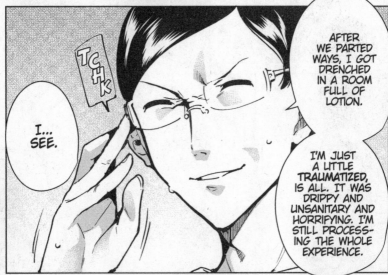

TCHK

AFTER WE PARTED WAYS, I GOT DRENCHED IN A ROOM FULL OF LOTION.

I... SEE.

I'M JUST A LITTLE *TRAUMATIZED*, IS ALL. IT WAS DRIPPY AND UNSANITARY AND HORRIFYING. I'M STILL PROCESSING THE WHOLE EXPERIENCE.

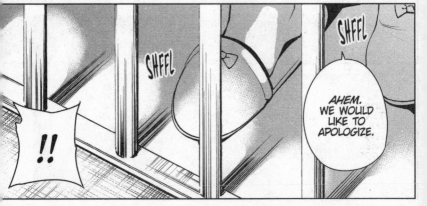

SHFFL

SHFFL

!!

AHEM. WE WOULD LIKE TO APOLOGIZE.

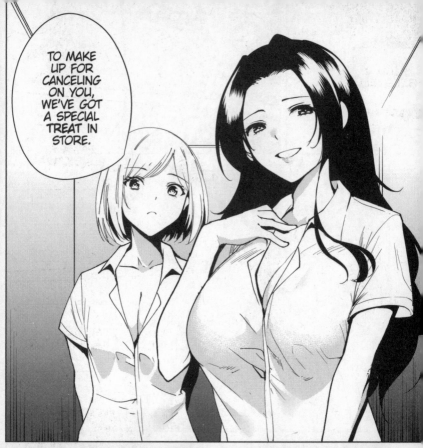

TO MAKE UP FOR CANCELING ON YOU, WE'VE GOT A SPECIAL TREAT IN STORE.

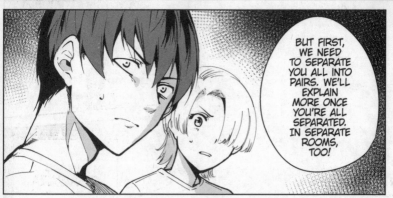

BUT FIRST, WE NEED TO SEPARATE YOU ALL INTO PAIRS. WE'LL EXPLAIN MORE ONCE YOU'RE ALL SEPARATED. IN SEPARATE ROOMS, TOO!

YO.
ERINA & FUJISHIRO
SAWA & SUKEKAWA
....
MITSUKO & KAZAMATSURI
SHKA
LET'S ENJOY OUR-SELVES. ♡
SAYAKA & IRABU
AINA & OGAWARA
M-M-ME?!

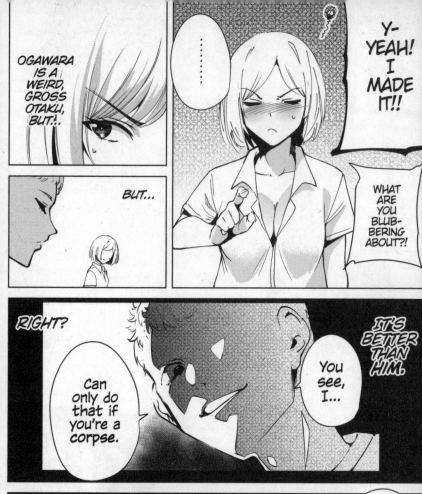

OGAWARA IS A WEIRD, GROSS OTAKU, BUT...

BUT...

. . . . . .

Y-YEAH! I MADE IT!!

WHAT ARE YOU BLUBBERING ABOUT?!

RIGHT?

Can only do that if you're a corpse.

You see, I...

IT'S BETTER THAN HIM.

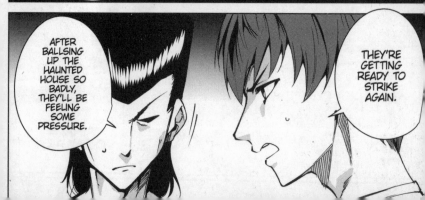

AFTER BALLSING UP THE HAUNTED HOUSE SO BADLY, THEY'LL BE FEELING SOME PRESSURE.

THEY'RE GETTING READY TO STRIKE AGAIN.

YEAH!!

WE CAN GET THROUGH THIS!!

NO MATTER WHAT HAPPENS, PROTECT YOUR VIRGINITY!

THIS IS GOING TO BE A HARD PUSH!

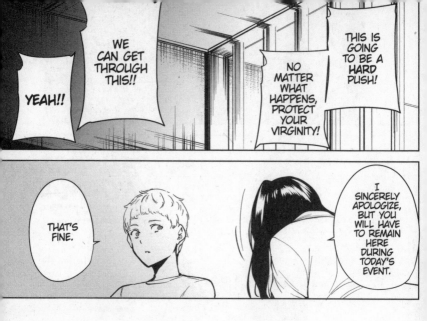

THAT'S FINE.

I SINCERELY APOLOGIZE, BUT YOU WILL HAVE TO REMAIN HERE DURING TODAY'S EVENT.

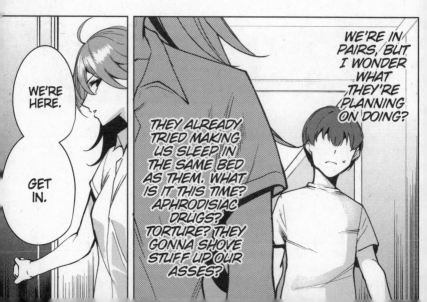

WE'RE HERE.

GET IN.

THEY ALREADY TRIED MAKING US SLEEP IN THE SAME BED AS THEM. WHAT IS IT THIS TIME? APHRODISIAC DRUGS? TORTURE? THEY GONNA SHOVE STUFF UP OUR ASSES?

WE'RE IN PAIRS, BUT I WONDER WHAT THEY'RE PLANNING ON DOING?

IT'S A...
PERFECTLY NORMAL BED?
AND A PHONE?

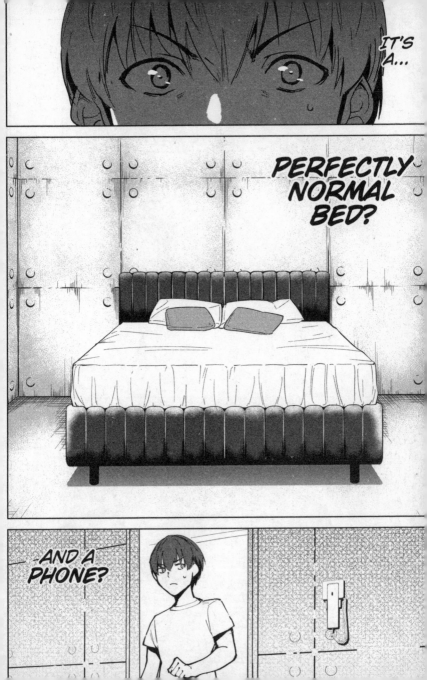

THERE ARE NO CAMERAS OR ANY-THING.
IT'S A SECRET ROOM!
THERE APPEARS TO BE SOME COLLUSION AFOOT.
SOMEONE HAS BEEN TIPPING YOU ALL OFF. SO WE'VE TAKEN... CERTAIN MEASURES.
IN HERE?
THERE IS NO WAY FOR YOU TO KNOW WHAT EVERYONE ELSE IS DOING. NO LIFELINES.
NO MATTER WHAT YOU DO WITH ME...
NO ONE WILL BE ANY WISER FOR IT.

SO, IF YOU JUST DO IT QUICKLY NOW...
THERE'S NO WAY WE'LL BE CAUGHT.
...
CREEEAK
RIGHT? ♡
FSHH

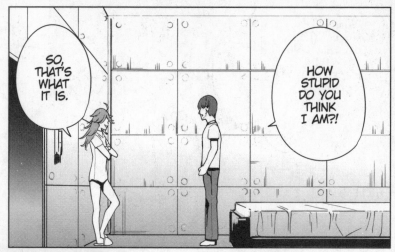

SO, THAT'S WHAT IT IS.

HOW STUPID DO YOU THINK I AM?!

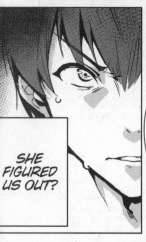

SHE FIGURED US OUT?

OR SOME NON-SENSE LIKE THAT, RIGHT?

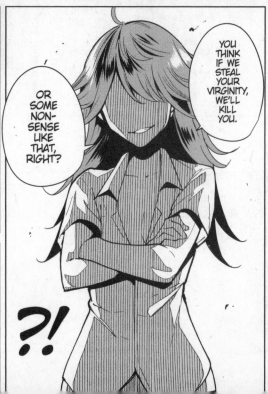

YOU THINK IF WE STEAL YOUR VIRGINITY, WE'LL KILL YOU.

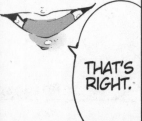

THAT'S RIGHT.

?!

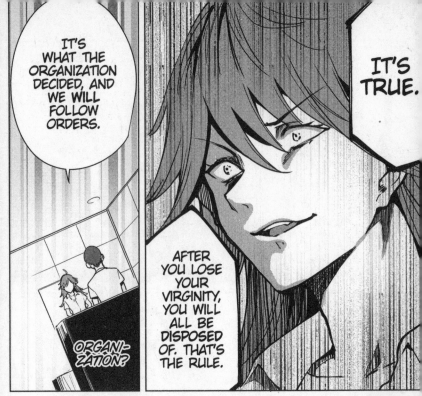

IT'S WHAT THE ORGANIZATION DECIDED, AND WE WILL FOLLOW ORDERS.

IT'S TRUE.

AFTER YOU LOSE YOUR VIRGINITY, YOU WILL ALL BE DISPOSED OF. THAT'S THE RULE.

ORGANI-ZATION?

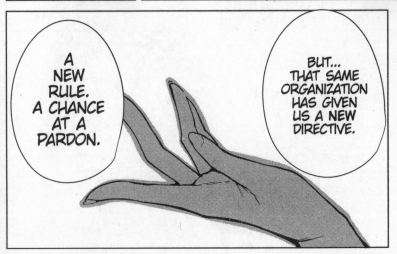

A NEW RULE. A CHANCE AT A PARDON.

BUT... THAT SAME ORGANIZATION HAS GIVEN US A NEW DIRECTIVE.

WE WILL LET YOU WALTZ OUT OF THIS PRISON ALIVE.
BUT...
THAT ONLY APPLIES IF YOU GIVE UP YOUR VIRGINITY IMME-DIATELY.

BUT WAIT. THERE'S MORE!
ALL FIVE OF YOU ARE IN THE EXACT SAME SITUATION.
BUT ONLY THE FIRST THREE OF YOU TO TAKE THIS OPTION WILL RECEIVE YOUR FREEDOM.
SO HOW ABOUT IT? COME IN ME, GO OUT THERE.
POSE
YOU WANT TO GO, RIGHT? I'LL HELP YOU... GO.

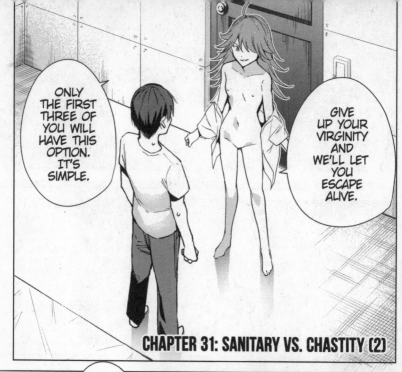

ONLY THE FIRST THREE OF YOU WILL HAVE THIS OPTION. IT'S SIMPLE.

GIVE UP YOUR VIRGINITY AND WE'LL LET YOU ESCAPE ALIVE.

CHAPTER 31: SANITARY VS. CHASTITY (2)

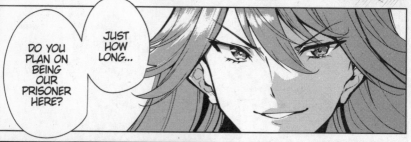

DO YOU PLAN ON BEING OUR PRISONER HERE?

JUST HOW LONG...

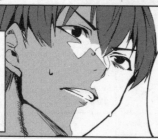

WAIT! I KNOW WHAT THIS IS!

YOUR WINDOW OF OPPORTUNITY IS CLOSING. WHAT WILL IT BE?

IF YOU AREN'T QUICK ENOUGH, YOU'LL GET LEFT BEHIND.

THE PRISONER'S DILEMMA!

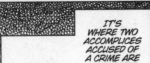

IT'S A WELL-KNOWN CONCEPT IN GAME THEORY.

IT'S WHERE TWO ACCOMPLICES ACCUSED OF A CRIME ARE SEPARATED AND INTERROGATED IN SEPARATE ROOMS.

THEY ARE GIVEN THE CHOICE TO EITHER CONFESS OR REMAIN SILENT.

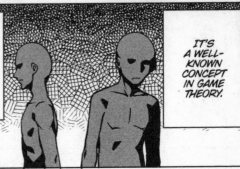

FOR EXAMPLE, IF ONE OF THEM DECIDES TO CONFESS WHILE THE OTHER REMAINS SILENT...

THE ONE WHO CONFESSES IS RELEASED ON A PLEA BARGAIN. HOWEVER...

THE ONE WHO REMAINED SILENT GETS AN EVEN LONGER SENTENCE. LET'S SAY FIVE YEARS.

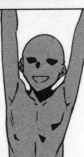

THE MOST FAVORABLE OUTCOME FOR THE WHOLE... IS FOR BOTH PARTIES TO REMAIN SILENT.

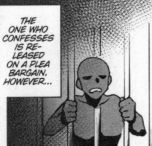

		Perpetrator A	
		Confess	Remain Silent
Perpetrator B — Confess		3 years / 3 years	5 years / 0 years (Release)
Perpetrator B — Remain Silent		0 years (Release) / 5 years	1 year / 1 year

IF THEY BOTH CONFESSED, EACH WOULD RECEIVE THREE YEARS; IF THEY BOTH REMAINED SILENT, EACH WOULD ONLY RECEIVE ONE YEAR.

HOWEVER, FOR THE INDIVIDUAL, THE BEST OPTION WOULD BE TO CONFESS.
WHETHER THEY CHOOSE TO CONFESS OR REMAIN SILENT, THE OPTION THAT HAS THE BEST RETURN... THAT MAKES THE MOST SENSE FOR THE INDIVIDUAL... IS TO CONFESS.
Perpetrator A
Confess
Remain Silent
Perpetrator B
Confess
Remain Silent
3 years
<
5 years
0 years (Release)
<
1 year
HOWEVER, IF BOTH INDIVIDUALS CHOOSE TO CONFESS, THEN THEY BOTH LOSE. THIS IS WHY IT IS CALLED THE PRISONER'S DILEMMA.
DOES THAT MEAN IN THIS CASE... THE MOST LOGICAL OPTION WOULD BE TO THROW AWAY MY VIRGINITY??
HEY, EARTH TO BRAIN GENIUS. YOU'RE RUNNING OUT OF TIME.
AH... THAT'S RIGHT.
SMIRK

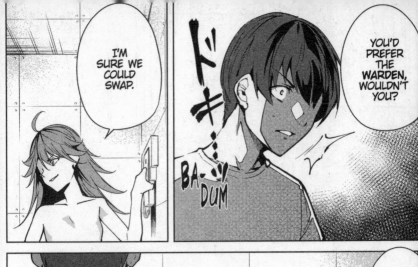

I'M SURE WE COULD SWAP.

YOU'D PREFER THE WARDEN, WOULDN'T YOU?

ド キ......

BA- DUM

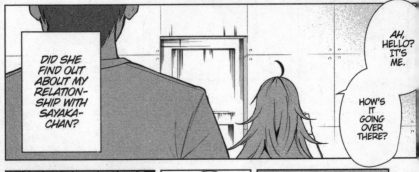

DID SHE FIND OUT ABOUT MY RELATIONSHIP WITH SAYAKA-CHAN?

AH, HELLO? IT'S ME.

HOW'S IT GOING OVER THERE?

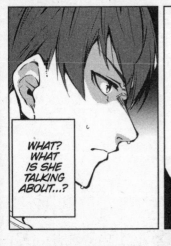

WHAT? WHAT IS SHE TALKING ABOUT...?

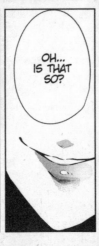

OH... IS THAT SO?

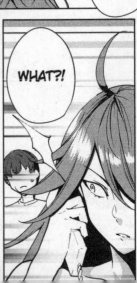

WHAT?!

ONE OF YOU HAS ALREADY DONE IT.

!!

KER-CHAK

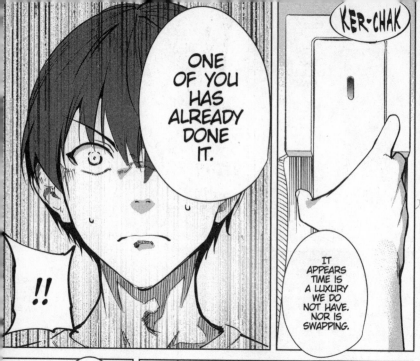

IT APPEARS TIME IS A LUXURY WE DO NOT HAVE. NOR IS SWAPPING.

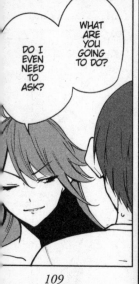

DO I EVEN NEED TO ASK?

WHAT ARE YOU GOING TO DO?

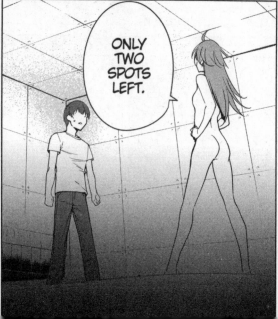

ONLY TWO SPOTS LEFT.

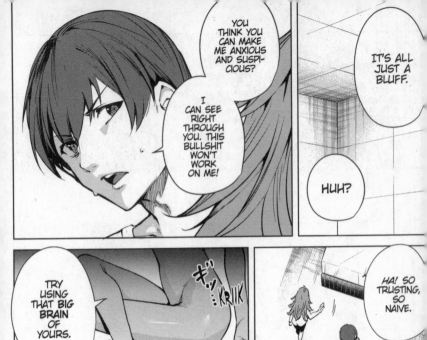

YOU THINK YOU CAN MAKE ME ANXIOUS AND SUSPICIOUS?

I CAN SEE RIGHT THROUGH YOU. THIS BULLSHIT WON'T WORK ON ME!

IT'S ALL JUST A BLUFF.

HUH?

TRY USING THAT BIG BRAIN OF YOURS.

ギ"ッ...KRIIK

HA! SO TRUSTING, SO NAIVE.

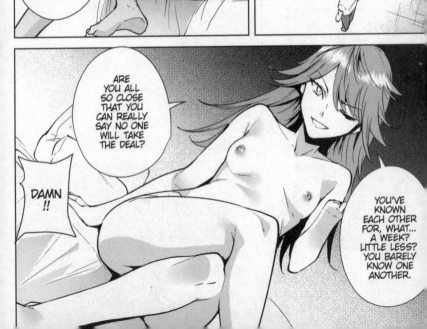

ARE YOU ALL SO CLOSE THAT YOU CAN REALLY SAY NO ONE WILL TAKE THE DEAL?

DAMN!!

YOU'VE KNOWN EACH OTHER FOR, WHAT... A WEEK? LITTLE LESS? YOU BARELY KNOW ONE ANOTHER.

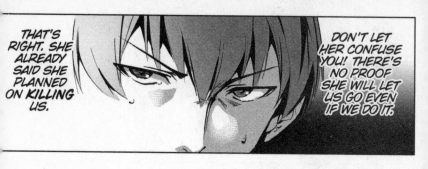

THAT'S RIGHT. SHE ALREADY SAID SHE PLANNED ON **KILLING** US.

DON'T LET HER CONFUSE YOU!! THERE'S NO PROOF SHE WILL LET US GO EVEN IF WE DO IT.

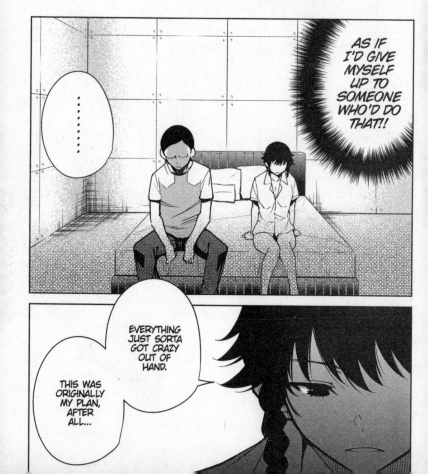

AS IF I'D GIVE MYSELF UP TO SOMEONE WHO'D DO THAT!!

· · · · · · ·

EVERYTHING JUST SORTA GOT CRAZY OUT OF HAND.

THIS WAS ORIGINALLY MY PLAN, AFTER ALL...

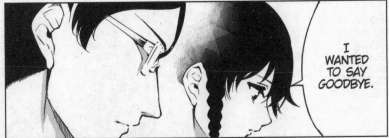

I WANTED TO SAY GOODBYE.

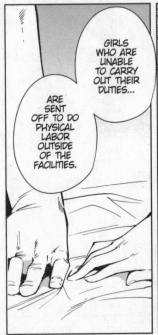

GIRLS WHO ARE UNABLE TO CARRY OUT THEIR DUTIES...

ARE SENT OFF TO DO PHYSICAL LABOR OUTSIDE OF THE FACILITIES.

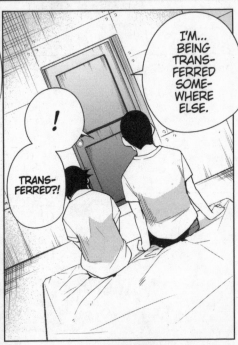

I'M... BEING TRANS- FERRED SOME- WHERE ELSE.

!

TRANS- FERRED?!

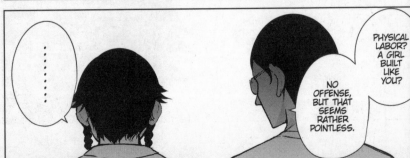

......

NO OFFENSE, BUT THAT SEEMS RATHER POINTLESS.

PHYSICAL LABOR? A GIRL BUILT LIKE YOU?

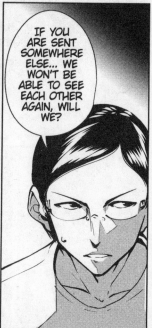

IF YOU ARE SENT SOMEWHERE ELSE... WE WON'T BE ABLE TO SEE EACH OTHER AGAIN, WILL WE?

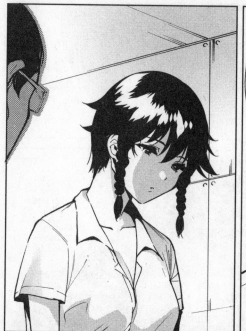

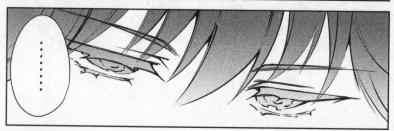

. . . .

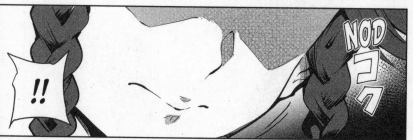

!!

NOD
コク

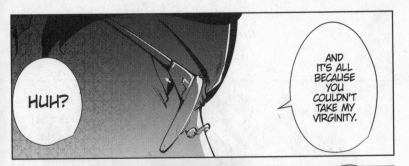

AND IT'S ALL BECAUSE YOU COULDN'T TAKE MY VIRGINITY.

HUH?

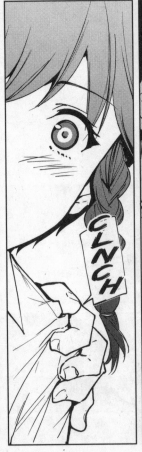

CLNCH

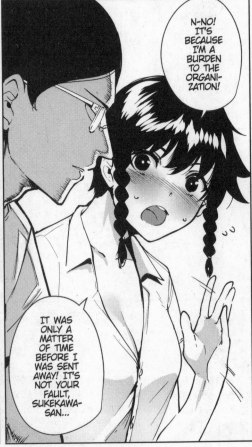

N-NO! IT'S BECAUSE I'M A BURDEN TO THE ORGANIZATION!

IT WAS ONLY A MATTER OF TIME BEFORE I WAS SENT AWAY! IT'S NOT YOUR FAULT, SUKEKAWA-SAN...

BA-DUM
CLNCH
ク
ST... STOP... SUKE-KAWA... SAN...!
I WANT TO DO IT.

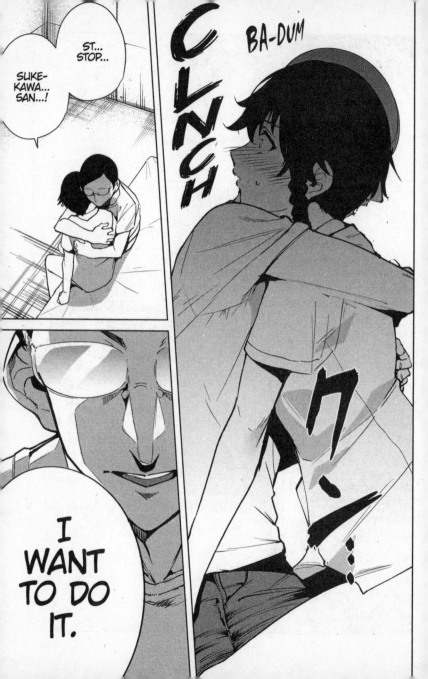

I DON'T CARE WHAT HAPPENS TO ME.
NO MATTER WHAT...
KA-THUMP
I... I WANT YOU!

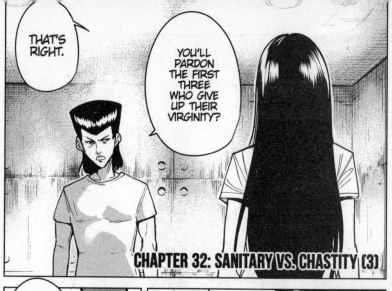

THAT'S RIGHT.

YOU'LL PARDON THE FIRST THREE WHO GIVE UP THEIR VIRGINITY?

CHAPTER 32: SANITARY VS. CHASTITY (3)

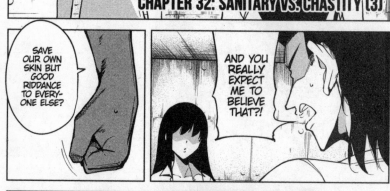

SAVE OUR OWN SKIN BUT GOOD RIDDANCE TO EVERYONE ELSE?

AND YOU REALLY EXPECT ME TO BELIEVE THAT?!

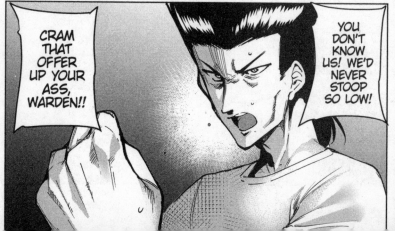

CRAM THAT OFFER UP YOUR ASS, WARDEN!!

YOU DON'T KNOW US! WE'D NEVER STOOP SO LOW!

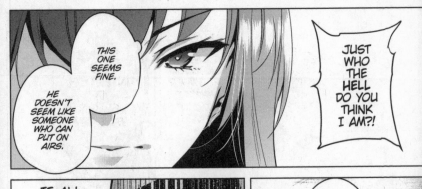

THIS ONE SEEMS FINE.

HE DOESN'T SEEM LIKE SOMEONE WHO CAN PUT ON AIRS.

JUST WHO THE HELL DO YOU THINK I AM?!

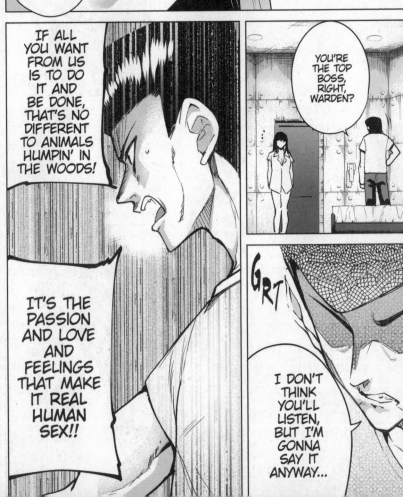

IF ALL YOU WANT FROM US IS TO DO IT AND BE DONE, THAT'S NO DIFFERENT TO ANIMALS HUMPIN' IN THE WOODS!

IT'S THE PASSION AND LOVE AND FEELINGS THAT MAKE IT REAL HUMAN SEX!!

YOU'RE THE TOP BOSS, RIGHT, WARDEN?

GRT!

I DON'T THINK YOU'LL LISTEN, BUT I'M GONNA SAY IT ANYWAY...

AND I HAVE NO INTENTION OF SIMPLY MATING!
THAT'S RIGHT...
SOME-DAY, WHEN I FIND A PARTNER THAT I TRULY LOVE...
MY IMPOTENCE WILL FINALLY BE GONE!!
IT'S THE LOVE, HUH?
......
SO, AS LONG AS THERE IS...
LOVE ...?

I WANT YOU.
I... LOVE YOU!
......
BLUSH

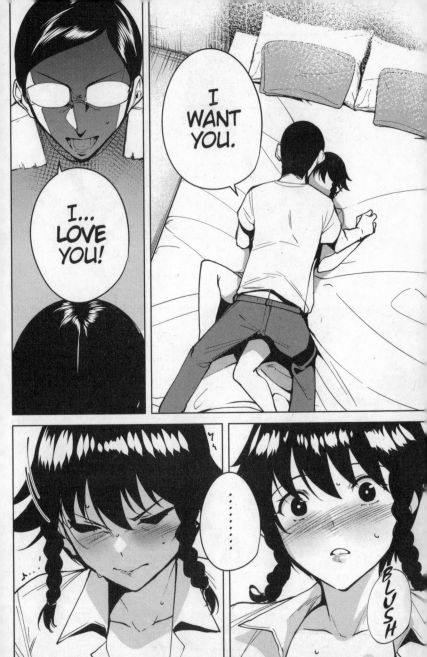

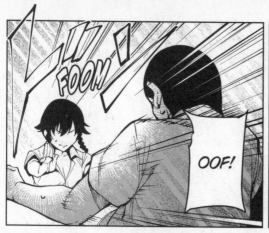

FOOM!

OOF!

SHFF

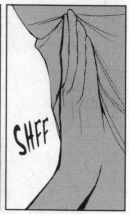

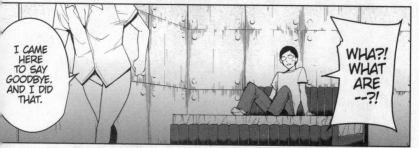

I CAME HERE TO SAY GOODBYE. AND I DID THAT.

WHA?! WHAT ARE --?!

GOODBYE, SUKE-KAWA-SAN.

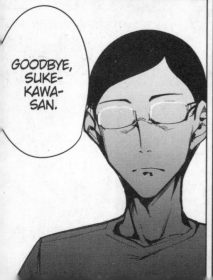

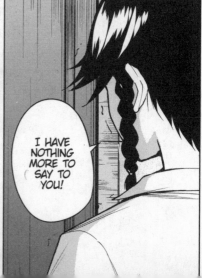

I HAVE NOTHING MORE TO SAY TO YOU!

IF WE MAKE LOVE...
KLAK
I WILL BE KILLED, WON'T I?
!...
YES. THAT'S RIGHT.

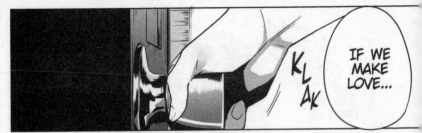

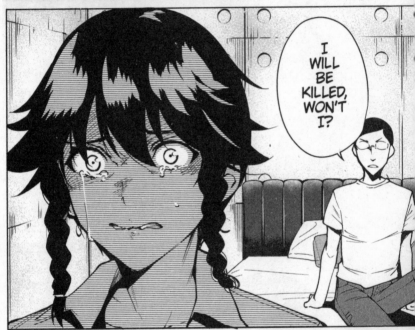

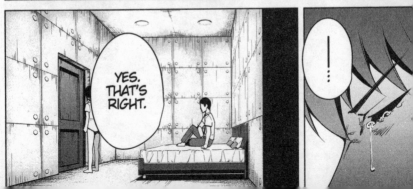

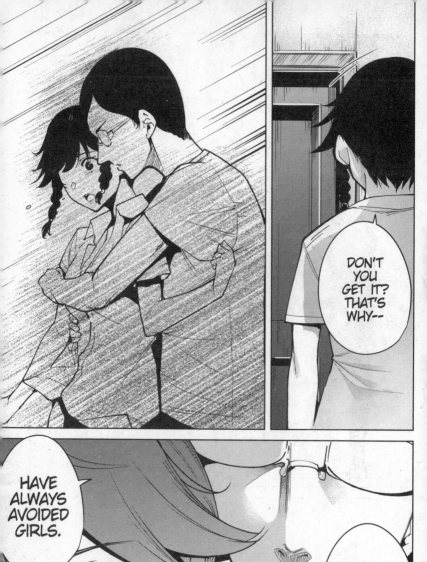

DON'T YOU GET IT? THAT'S WHY--

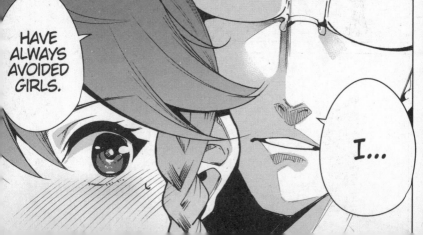

HAVE ALWAYS AVOIDED GIRLS.

I...

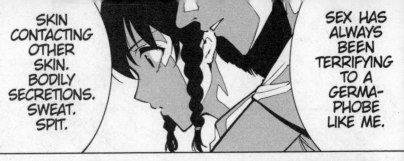

SKIN CONTACTING OTHER SKIN. BODILY SECRETIONS. SWEAT. SPIT.

SEX HAS ALWAYS BEEN TERRIFYING TO A GERMA-PHOBE LIKE ME.

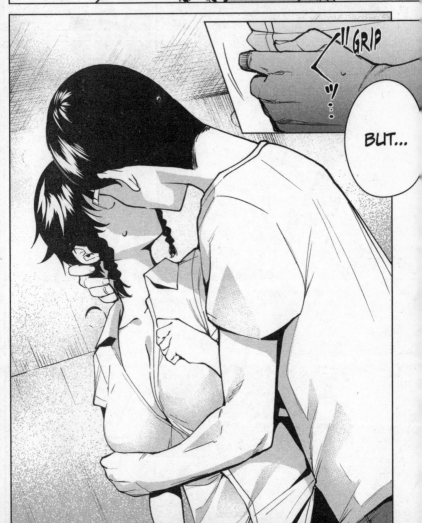

GRIP

BUT...

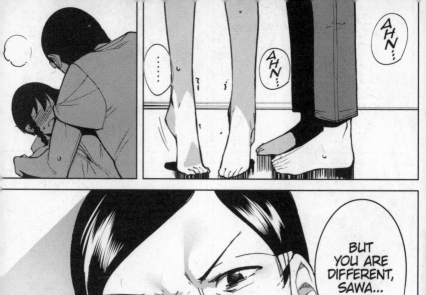

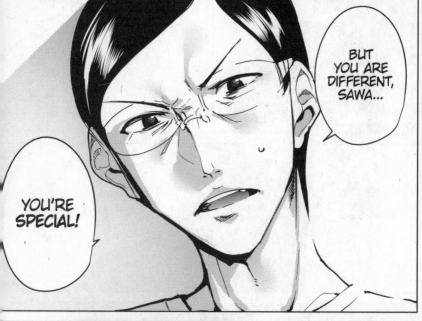

BUT YOU ARE DIFFERENT, SAWA...

YOU'RE SPECIAL!

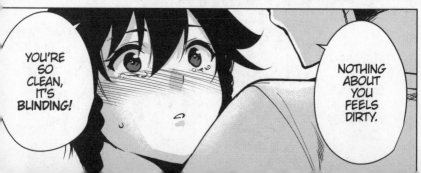

YOU'RE SO CLEAN, IT'S BLINDING!

NOTHING ABOUT YOU FEELS DIRTY.

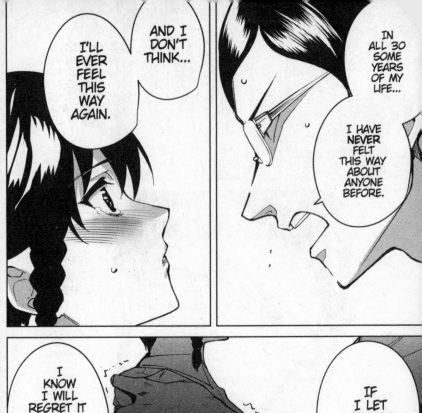

I'LL EVER FEEL THIS WAY AGAIN.

AND I DON'T THINK...

IN ALL 30 SOME YEARS OF MY LIFE...

I HAVE NEVER FELT THIS WAY ABOUT ANYONE BEFORE.

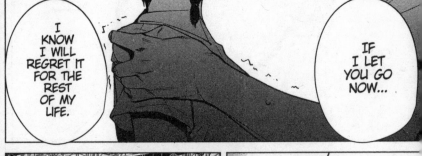

I KNOW I WILL REGRET IT FOR THE REST OF MY LIFE.

IF I LET YOU GO NOW...

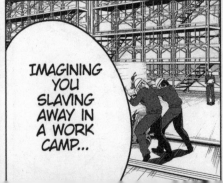

IMAGINING YOU SLAVING AWAY IN A WORK CAMP...

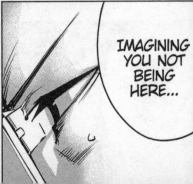

IMAGINING YOU NOT BEING HERE...

LIVING WITH ALL THAT PAIN DOESN'T SOUND LIKE MUCH OF A LIFE.
HOW MUCH LONGER WOULD THEY LET ME LIVE HERE, ANYWAY? EVERY DAY WOULD BE TORTURE.
I AM PREPARED TO DIE HAVING LOVED YOU...
THAN TO LIVE IN A WORLD WHERE YOU ARE NOT WITH ME!

SAWA! I LIKE YOU!
NO-- NO, I LOVE YOU! ENOUGH TO DIE TO BE WITH YOU!

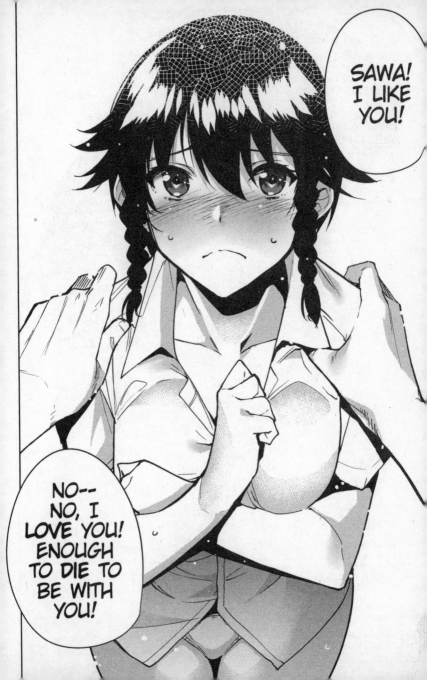

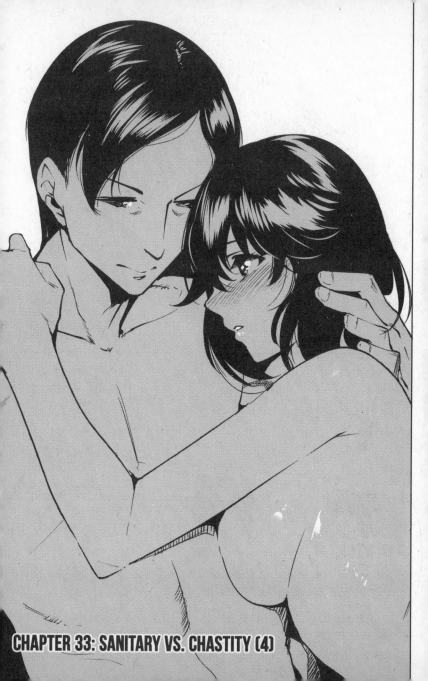

CHAPTER 33: SANITARY VS. CHASTITY (4)

SAWA... I LOVE YOU.
I WANT TO MAKE LOVE WITH YOU.
EVEN IF IT MEANS I HAVE TO DIE!!
WHY...

I FINALLY GOT MY FEELINGS IN ORDER...
I HAD FINALLY DECIDED...
I HAD FINALLY DECIDED TO GIVE UP ON YOU.
WHY DO YOU HAVE TO SAY THAT NOW?

WITH ALL MY HEART!
I... I LOVE YOU, TOO!!

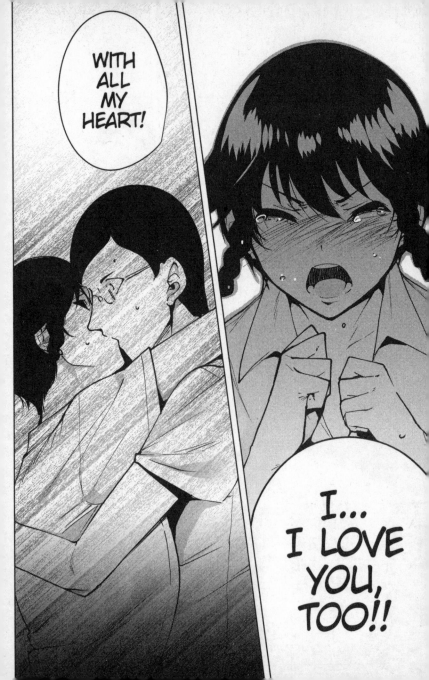

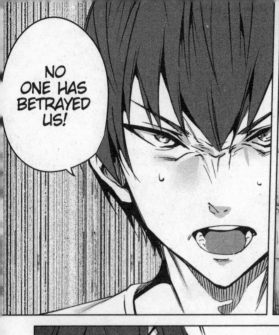

NO ONE HAS BETRAYED US!

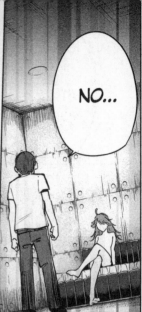

NO...

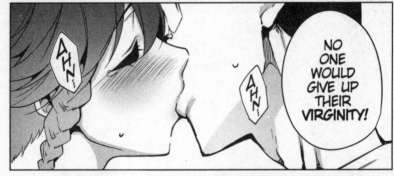

NO ONE WOULD GIVE UP THEIR VIRGINITY!

AHN...

AHN...

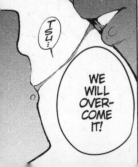

TSU...

WE WILL OVERCOME IT!

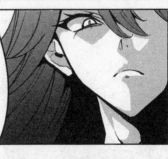

NO MATTER WHAT TRAP YOU MAY LAY BEFORE US...

THIS ISN'T SOMETHING YOU CAN DO WITH JUST ANYONE.
HAHH...
HAHH...
SHIFF
HAHH...
THERE IS A PASSION AND HAPPINESS THAT COMES WITH THAT CONNECTION. WITH SHARING YOURSELF WITH SOMEONE YOU CARE ABOUT!
HEH...
PANT...
むにゅ…
YES...
SHLIP

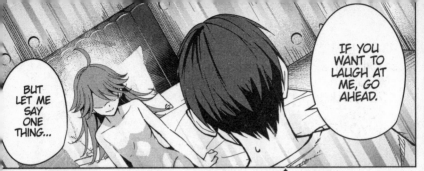

IF YOU WANT TO LAUGH AT ME, GO AHEAD.

BUT LET ME SAY ONE THING...

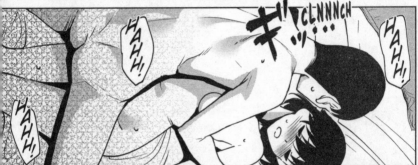

HAHH!

HAHH!

HAHH!

HAHH!

#!'CLNNNCH...

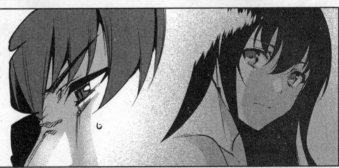

I MADE A PROMISE TO SOME- ONE WHO MATTERS FAR, FAR MORE TO ME THAN YOU!!

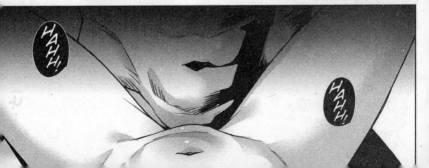

HAHH!

HAHH!

DON'T UNDER-ESTIMATE US VIRGINS!
THUD
JOLT
AH! ♥
IS THAT SO?

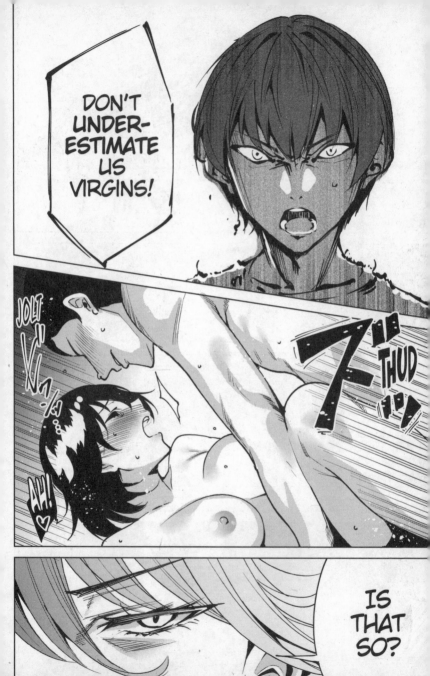

WHERE ARE YOU GOING?!
FWSH
YOU ARE A POINTLESS DWEEB AND BEING HERE IS A WASTE OF MY TIME.
YOU'RE GOING TO REGRET THIS.
KER-CHAK
REGRET ...?
YEAH, RIGHT.
CLINCH

I COULD NEVER REGRET THIS!
HUFF...
HUFF...

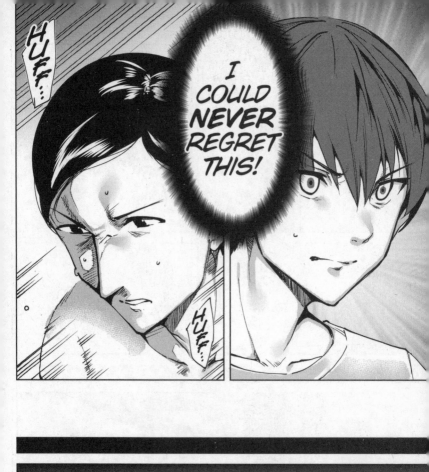

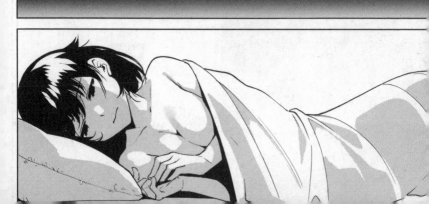

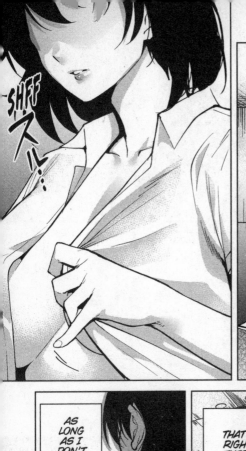

SHFF
スルッ...

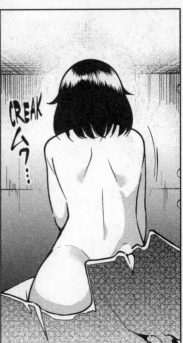

CREAK
ムフ？...

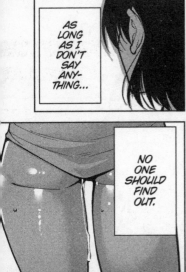

AS LONG AS I DON'T SAY ANYTHING...

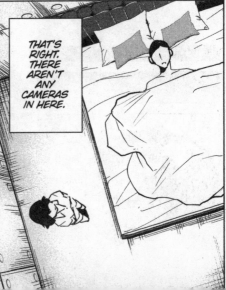

THAT'S RIGHT. THERE AREN'T ANY CAMERAS IN HERE.

NO ONE SHOULD FIND OUT.

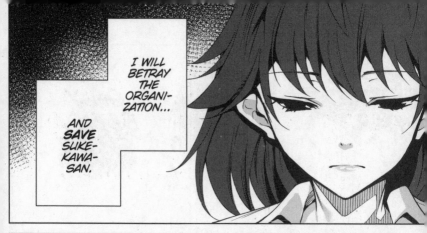

I WILL BETRAY THE ORGANI- ZATION...

AND SAVE SUKE- KAWA- SAN.

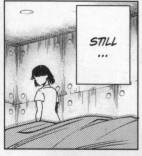

STILL ...

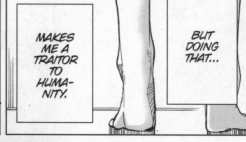

MAKES ME A TRAITOR TO HUMA- NITY.

BUT DOING THAT...

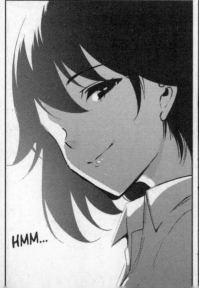

HMM...

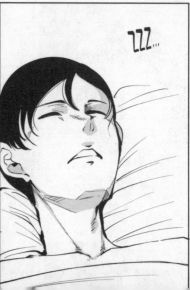

ZZZ...

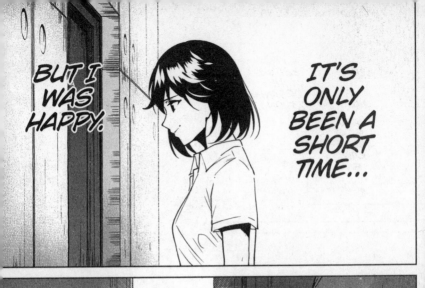

BUT I WAS HAPPY.

IT'S ONLY BEEN A SHORT TIME...

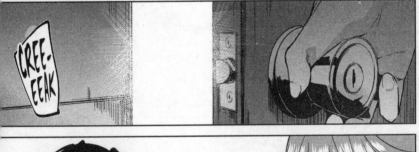

CREE-EEAK

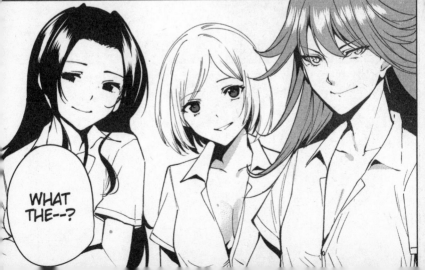

WHAT THE--?

CON-GRATULA-TIONS, SAWA-SAN!
YOU DID IT, SAWA-CHAN!

HUH ?!

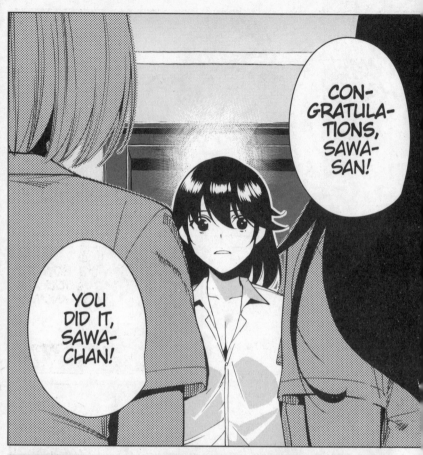

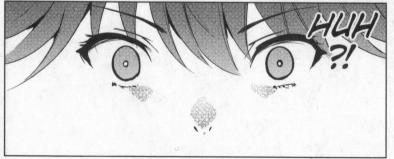

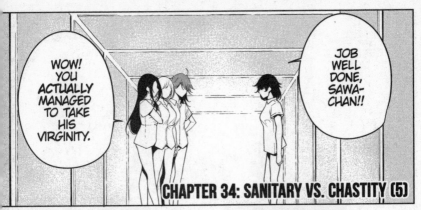

WOW! YOU ACTUALLY MANAGED TO TAKE HIS VIRGINITY.

JOB WELL DONE, SAWA-CHAN!!

CHAPTER 34: SANITARY VS. CHASTITY (5)

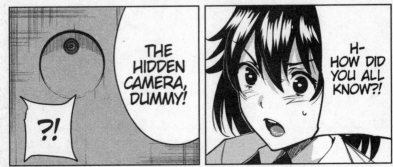

THE HIDDEN CAMERA, DUMMY!

?!

H-HOW DID YOU ALL KNOW?!

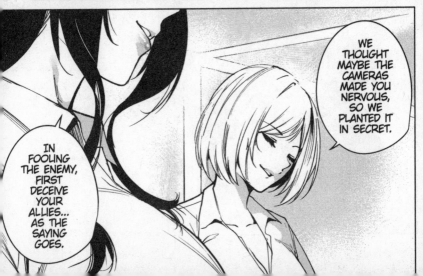

WE THOUGHT MAYBE THE CAMERAS MADE YOU NERVOUS, SO WE PLANTED IT IN SECRET.

IN FOOLING THE ENEMY, FIRST DECEIVE YOUR ALLIES... AS THE SAYING GOES.

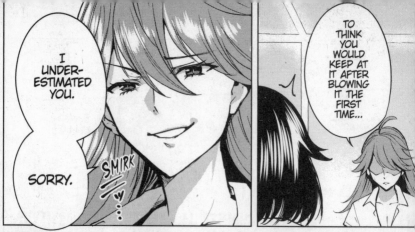

I UNDER-ESTIMATED YOU.

SORRY.

SMIRK

TO THINK YOU WOULD KEEP AT IT AFTER BLOWING IT THE FIRST TIME...

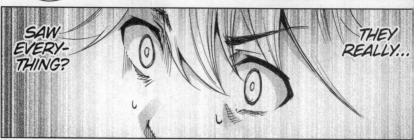

SAW EVERY-THING?

THEY REALLY...

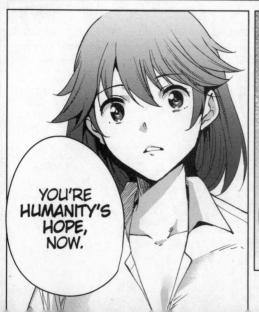

YOU'RE HUMANITY'S HOPE, NOW.

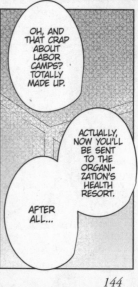

OH, AND THAT CRAP ABOUT LABOR CAMPS? TOTALLY MADE UP.

ACTUALLY, NOW YOU'LL BE SENT TO THE ORGANI-ZATION'S HEALTH RESORT.

AFTER ALL...

144

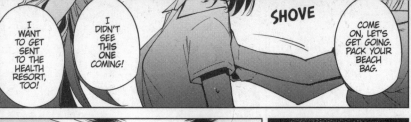

I WANT TO GET SENT TO THE HEALTH RESORT, TOO!

I DIDN'T SEE THIS ONE COMING!

SHOVE

COME ON, LET'S GET GOING. PACK YOUR BEACH BAG.

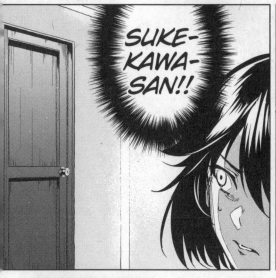

SUKE-KAWA-SAN!!

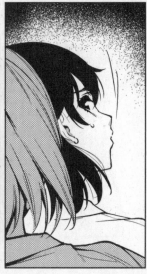

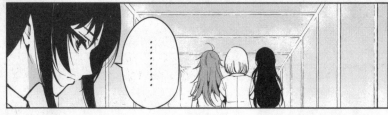

······

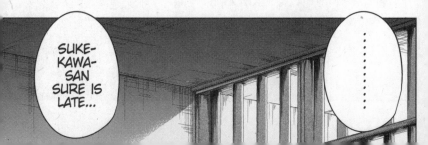

SUKE-KAWA-SAN SURE IS LATE...

······

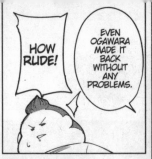

HOW RUDE!

EVEN OGAWARA MADE IT BACK WITHOUT ANY PROBLEMS.

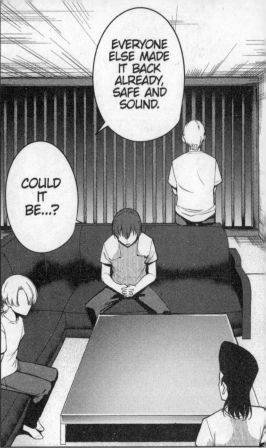

EVERYONE ELSE MADE IT BACK ALREADY, SAFE AND SOUND.

COULD IT BE...?

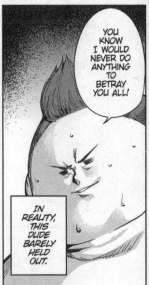

YOU KNOW I WOULD NEVER DO ANYTHING TO BETRAY YOU ALL!

IN REALITY, THIS DUDE BARELY HELD OUT.

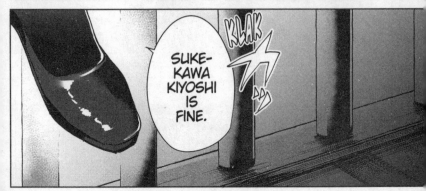

SUKE-KAWA KIYOSHI IS FINE.

KLAK

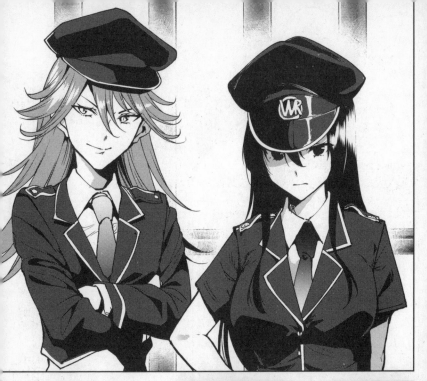

LAST NIGHT, HE TOOK OUR OFFER.

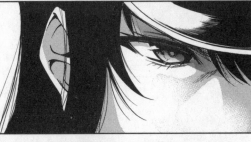

HE IS NO LONGER A VIRGIN.

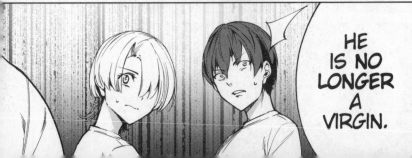

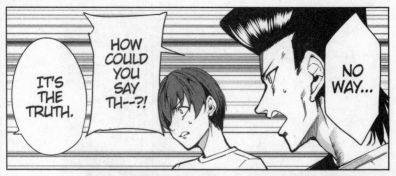

IT'S THE TRUTH.

HOW COULD YOU SAY TH--?!

NO WAY...

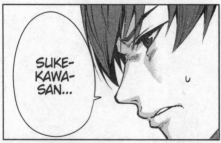

SUKE-KAWA-SAN...

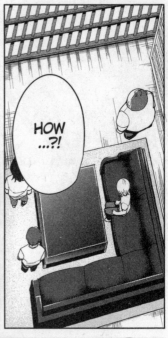

HOW ...?!

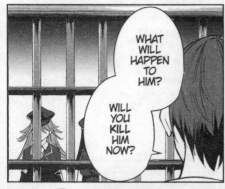

WHAT WILL HAPPEN TO HIM?

WILL YOU KILL HIM NOW?

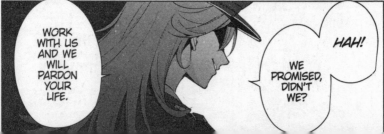

WORK WITH US AND WE WILL PARDON YOUR LIFE.

HAH!

WE PROMISED, DIDN'T WE?

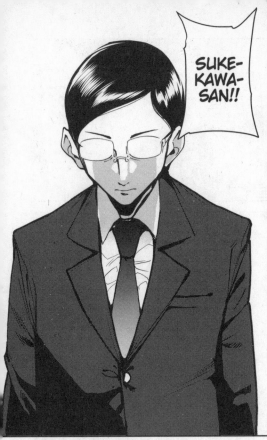

SUKE-KAWA-SAN!!

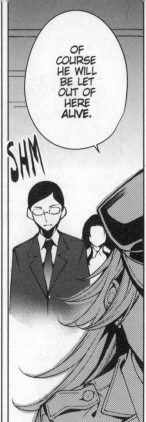

OF COURSE HE WILL BE LET OUT OF HERE ALIVE.

SHM

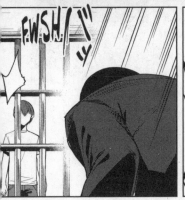

F.W.SH.!

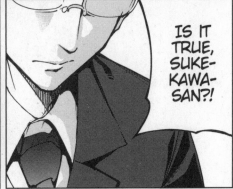

IS IT TRUE, SUKE-KAWA-SAN?!

I'M SORRY.
IT'S TRUE. I AM NO LONGER A VIRGIN.
BUT I DIDN'T KNOW ABOUT THE PLEA DEAL.
THOUGH I DIDN'T INTEND TO, IT SEEMS I AM ABOUT TO LEAVE YOU ALL BEHIND.

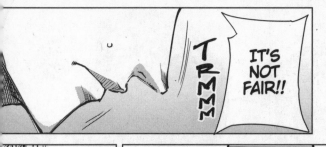

TRMMM

IT'S NOT FAIR!!

SUKE-KAWA...

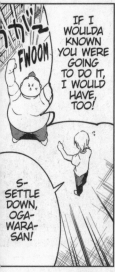

FWOOM

IF I WOULDA KNOWN YOU WERE GOING TO DO IT, I WOULD HAVE, TOO!

S-SETTLE DOWN, OGA-WARA-SAN!

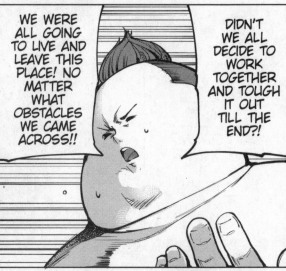

WE WERE ALL GOING TO LIVE AND LEAVE THIS PLACE! NO MATTER WHAT OBSTACLES WE CAME ACROSS!!

DIDN'T WE ALL DECIDE TO WORK TOGETHER AND TOUGH IT OUT TILL THE END?!

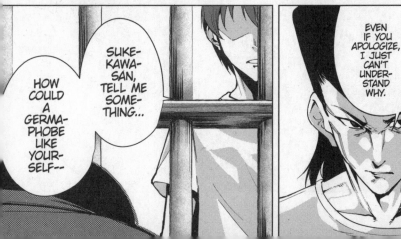

HOW COULD A GERMA-PHOBE LIKE YOUR-SELF--

SUKE-KAWA-SAN, TELL ME SOME-THING...

EVEN IF YOU APOLOGIZE, I JUST CAN'T UNDER-STAND WHY.

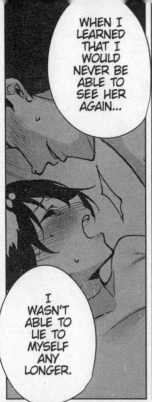

WHEN I LEARNED THAT I WOULD NEVER BE ABLE TO SEE HER AGAIN...

I WASN'T ABLE TO LIE TO MYSELF ANY LONGER.

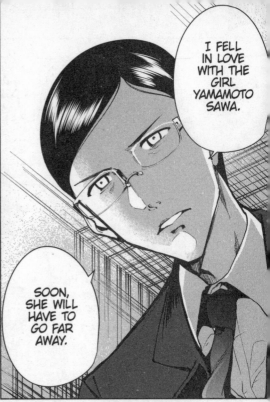

I FELL IN LOVE WITH THE GIRL YAMAMOTO SAWA.

SOON, SHE WILL HAVE TO GO FAR AWAY.

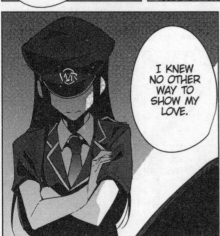

I KNEW NO OTHER WAY TO SHOW MY LOVE.

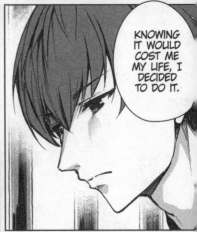

KNOWING IT WOULD COST ME MY LIFE, I DECIDED TO DO IT.

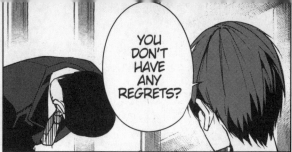

NONE.

EVEN IF THEY WERE TO KILL ME.

YOU DON'T HAVE ANY REGRETS?

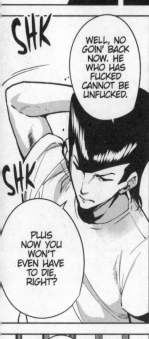

SHK

WELL, NO GOIN' BACK NOW. HE WHO HAS FUCKED CANNOT BE UNFUCKED.

SHK

PLUS NOW YOU WON'T EVEN HAVE TO DIE, RIGHT?

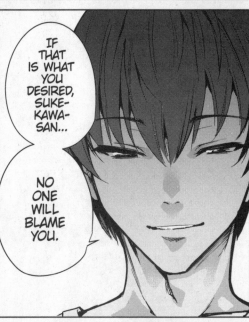

IF THAT IS WHAT YOU DESIRED, SUKE-KAWA-SAN...

NO ONE WILL BLAME YOU.

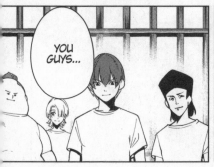

YOU GUYS...

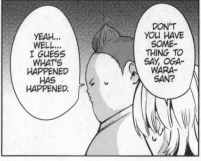

YEAH... WELL... I GUESS WHAT'S HAPPENED HAS HAPPENED.

DON'T YOU HAVE SOME-THING TO SAY, OGA-WARA-SAN?

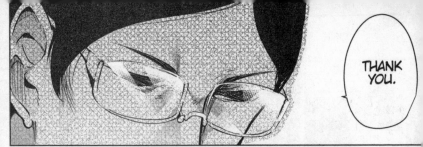

THANK YOU.

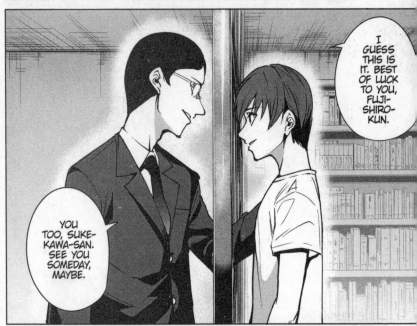

I GUESS THIS IS IT. BEST OF LUCK TO YOU, FUJI-SHIRO-KUN.

YOU TOO, SUKE-KAWA-SAN. SEE YOU SOMEDAY, MAYBE.

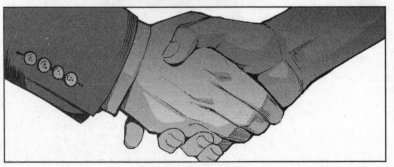

154

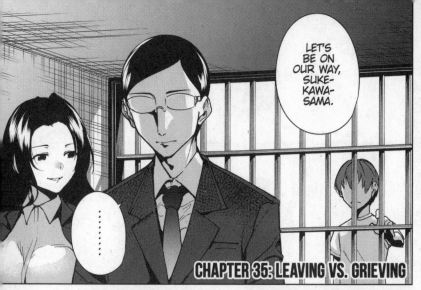

LET'S BE ON OUR WAY, SUKE-KAWA-SAMA.

・・・・・・・・・・

CHAPTER 35: LEAVING VS. GRIEVING

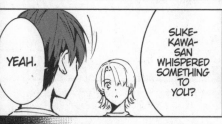

FUJI-SHIRO-KUN.

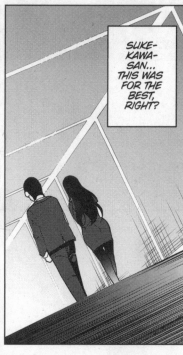

SUKE-KAWA-SAN... THIS WAS FOR THE BEST, RIGHT?

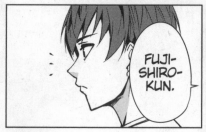

YEAH.

SUKE-KAWA-SAN WHISPERED SOMETHING TO YOU?

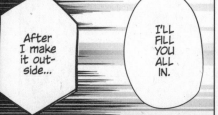

After I make it out-side...

I'LL FILL YOU ALL IN.

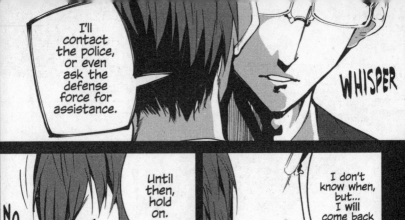

I'll contact the police, or even ask the defense force for assistance.

WHISPER

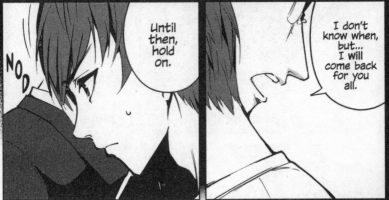

Until then, hold on.

NOD

I don't know when, but... I will come back for you all.

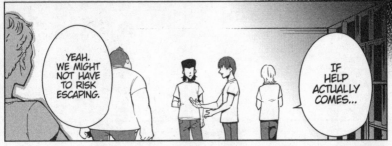

YEAH. WE MIGHT NOT HAVE TO RISK ESCAPING.

IF HELP ACTUALLY COMES...

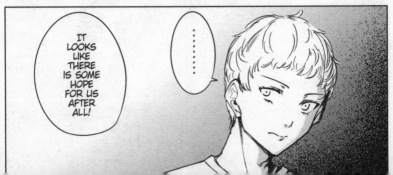

IT LOOKS LIKE THERE IS SOME HOPE FOR US AFTER ALL!

. . . . . .

CHF...
GO ON BY YOURSELF FROM HERE.
KEEP GOING STRAIGHT AND YOU'LL RUN INTO A DOOR.
ONCE WE'RE SURE YOU'RE THERE, THE DOOR WILL OPEN.
AS SOON AS IT OPENS, YOU'RE TO GO OUTSIDE. GOT IT?
YEAH.
SUKE-KAWA-SAN!

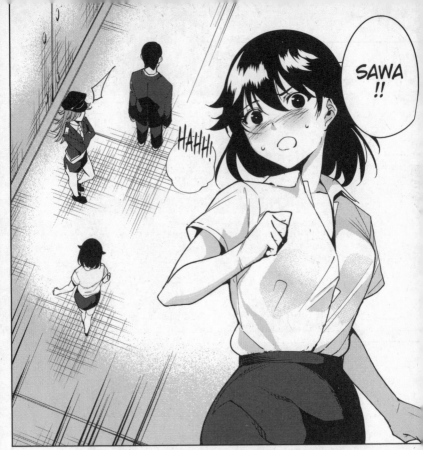

SAWA!!

HAHH!

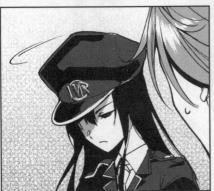

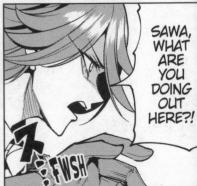

SAWA, WHAT ARE YOU DOING OUT HERE?!

FWSH

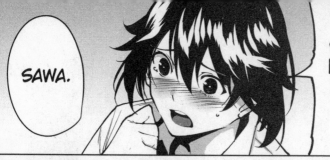

SAWA.

SUKE-KAWA-SAN... I...

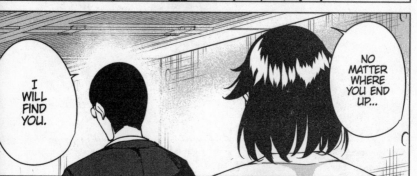

I WILL FIND YOU.

NO MATTER WHERE YOU END UP...

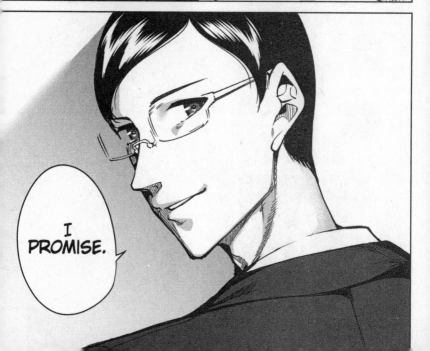

I PROMISE.

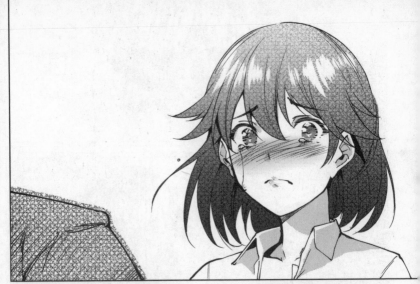

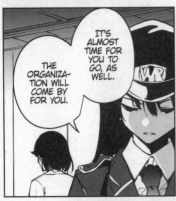

IT'S ALMOST TIME FOR YOU TO GO, AS WELL.

THE ORGANIZA-TION WILL COME BY FOR YOU.

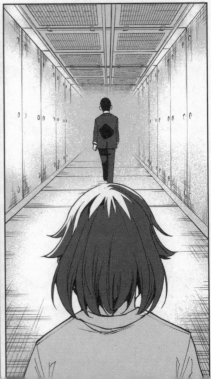

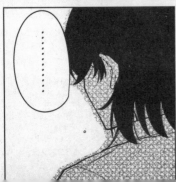

. . . .

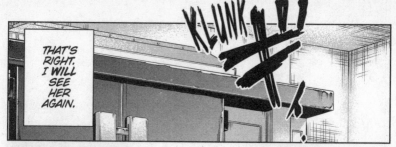

THAT'S RIGHT. I WILL SEE HER AGAIN.

KLUNK

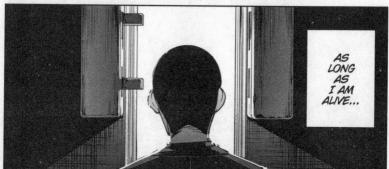

AS LONG AS I AM ALIVE...

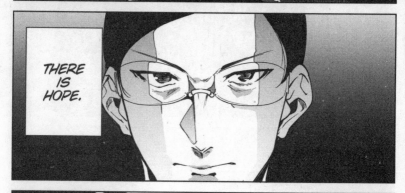

THERE IS HOPE.

WHAT...
WHAT...
THE HELL ?!

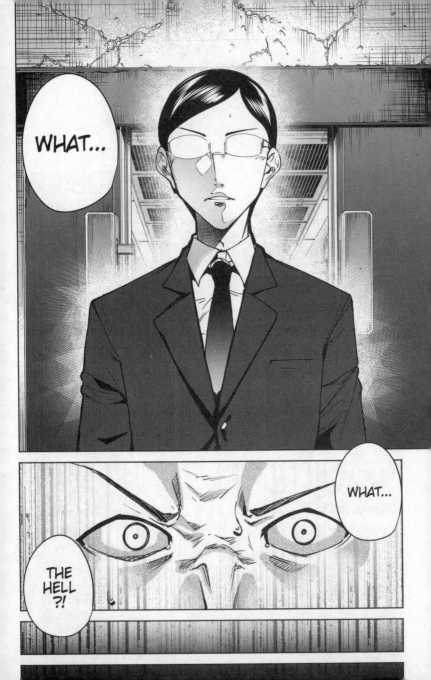

A FEW DAYS LATER...

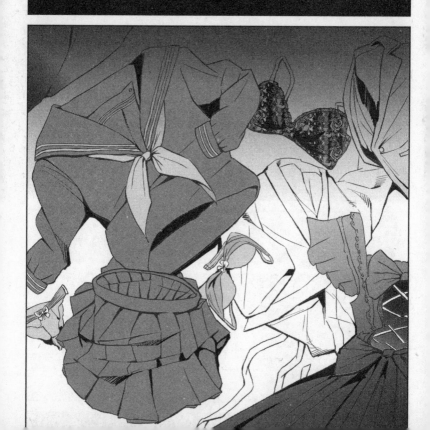

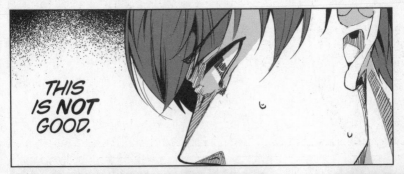

THIS IS NOT GOOD.

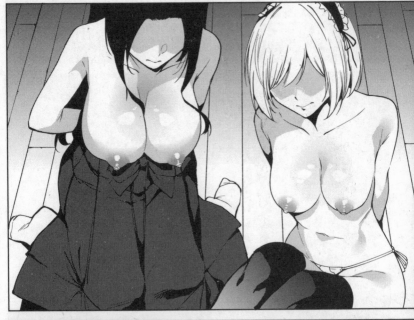

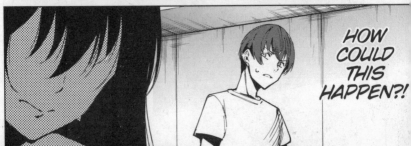

HOW COULD THIS HAPPEN?!

チャキ… CH-CHAK

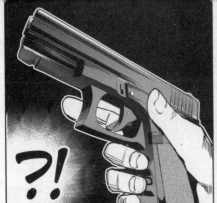

?!

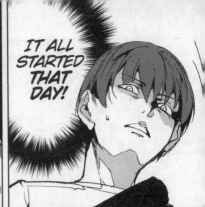

IT ALL STARTED THAT DAY!

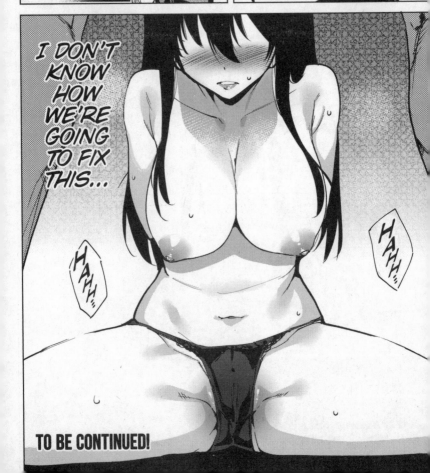

I DON'T KNOW HOW WE'RE GOING TO FIX THIS...

HAHH...

HAHH...

TO BE CONTINUED!

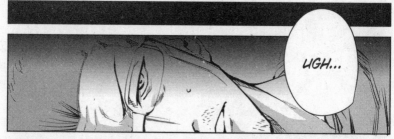

UGH...

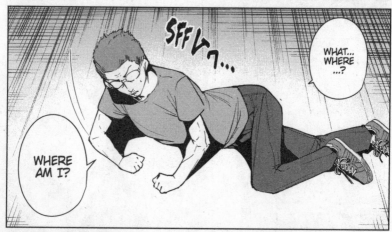

SFF レ٦...

WHAT... WHERE ...?

WHERE AM I?

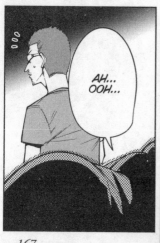

AH... OOH...

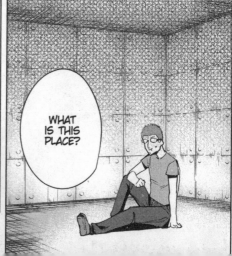

WHAT IS THIS PLACE?

ARE... ARE YOU OKAY?!
OOH...
HM? WHERE AM I?
I'M NOT SURE MYSELF. I JUST WOKE UP HERE.
WHER-EVER WE ARE, THERE AREN'T MANY EXITS.
WE'RE TRAPPED...
BUT, WHY?!

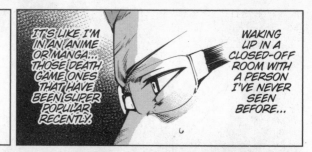

DEATH GAME??

IT'S LIKE I'M IN AN ANIME OR MANGA... THOSE DEATH GAME ONES THAT HAVE BEEN SUPER POPULAR RECENTLY.

WAKING UP IN A CLOSED-OFF ROOM WITH A PERSON I'VE NEVER SEEN BEFORE...

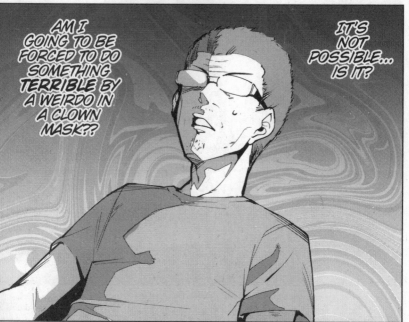

AM I GOING TO BE FORCED TO DO SOMETHING **TERRIBLE** BY A WEIRDO IN A CLOWN MASK??

IT'S NOT POSSIBLE... IS IT?

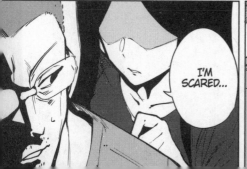

I'M SCARED...

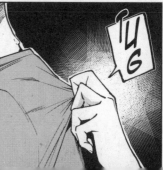

TUG

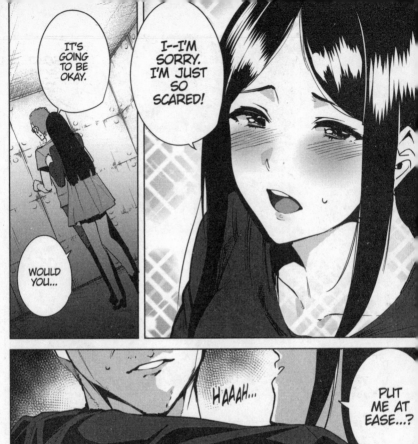

I--I'M SORRY. I'M JUST SO SCARED!
IT'S GOING TO BE OKAY.
WOULD YOU...
PUT ME AT EASE...?
HAAAH...
WHA ...?
MWA...♡
WHAT THE ABSOLUTE HELL?!
AHN...

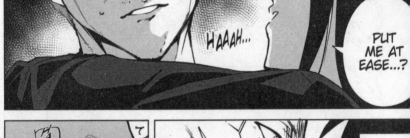

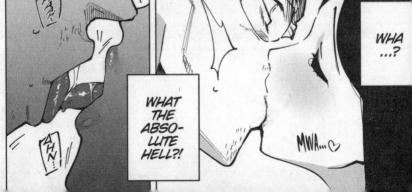

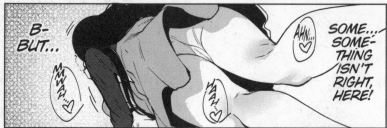

B-BUT...

AHN...♥

SOME... SOMETHING ISN'T RIGHT, HERE!

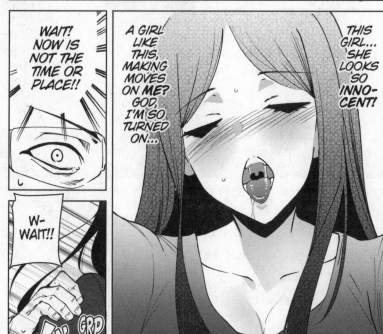

WAIT! NOW IS NOT THE TIME OR PLACE!!

W-WAIT!!

GRP

A GIRL LIKE THIS, MAKING MOVES ON ME? GOD, I'M SO TURNED ON...

THIS GIRL... SHE LOOKS SO INNOCENT!

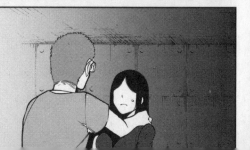

TMP

TMP

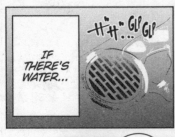

IF THERE'S WATER...

GLP GLP

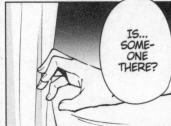

IS... SOME- ONE THERE?

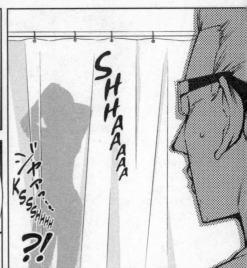

SHHAAAAA

KSSSSHHHH

?!

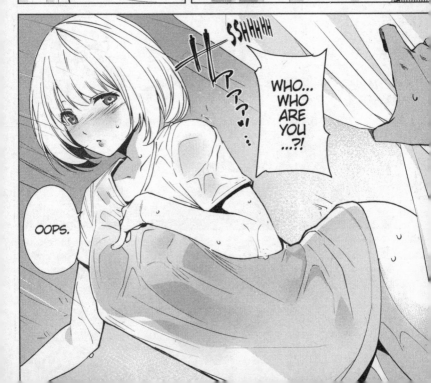

SSHHHHH

WHO... WHO ARE YOU ...?!

OOPS.

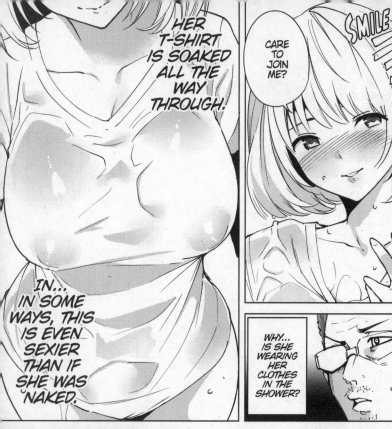

HER T-SHIRT IS SOAKED ALL THE WAY THROUGH!

IN... IN SOME WAYS, THIS IS EVEN SEXIER THAN IF SHE WAS NAKED.

CARE TO JOIN ME?

SMILE

WHY... IS SHE WEARING HER CLOTHES IN THE SHOWER?

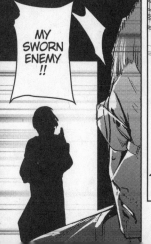

MY SWORN ENEMY!!

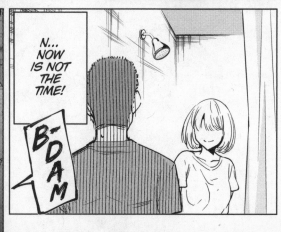

N... NOW IS NOT THE TIME!

B-DAM

THE TIME TO EXACT MY REVENGE HAS COME!!
ZA
HUH ?!
ZWA
PRE-PARE YOUR-SELF!!
FWOMP
DAMN... I WAS SUPPOSED TO EXACT MY REVENGE ...

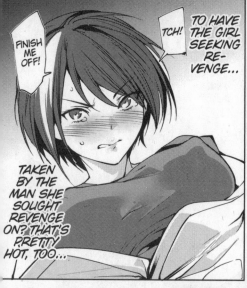

FINISH ME OFF!

TCH!

TO HAVE THE GIRL SEEKING REVENGE...

TAKEN BY THE MAN SHE SOUGHT REVENGE ON? THAT'S PRETTY HOT, TOO...

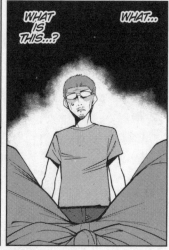

WHAT IS THIS...?

WHAT...

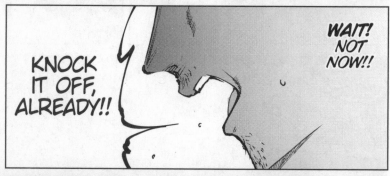

KNOCK IT OFF, ALREADY!!

WAIT! NOT NOW!!

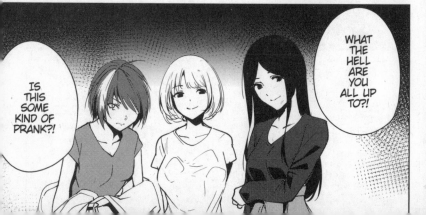

IS THIS SOME KIND OF PRANK?!

WHAT THE HELL ARE YOU ALL UP TO?!

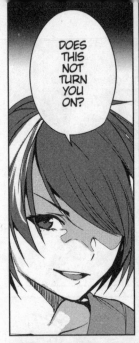

DOES THIS NOT TURN YOU ON?

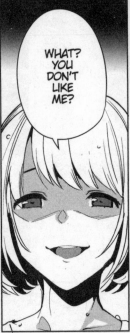

WHAT? YOU DON'T LIKE ME?

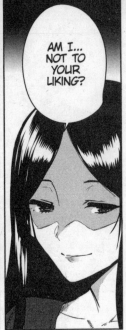

AM I... NOT TO YOUR LIKING?

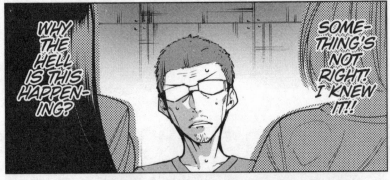

WHY THE HELL IS THIS HAPPEN-ING?

SOME-THING'S NOT RIGHT! I KNEW IT!!

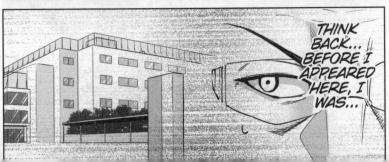

THINK BACK... BEFORE I APPEARED HERE, I WAS...

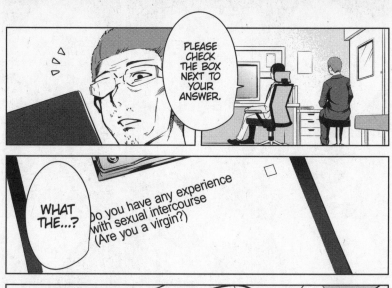

PLEASE CHECK THE BOX NEXT TO YOUR ANSWER.

WHAT THE...?

Do you have any experience with sexual intercourse (Are you a virgin?)

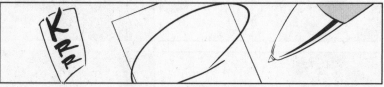

KRR

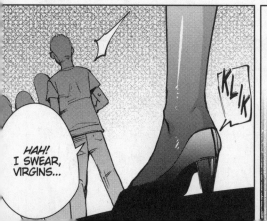

HAH! I SWEAR, VIRGINS...

KLIK

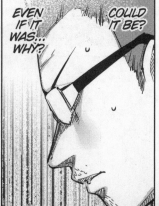

EVEN IF IT WAS... WHY?

COULD IT BE?

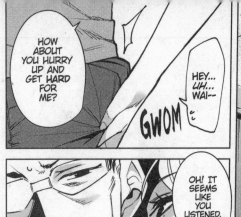

HOW ABOUT YOU HURRY UP AND GET HARD FOR ME?

HEY... UH... WAI--

GWOM

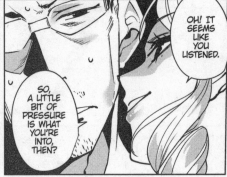

OH! IT SEEMS LIKE YOU LISTENED.

SO, A LITTLE BIT OF PRESSURE IS WHAT YOU'RE INTO, THEN?

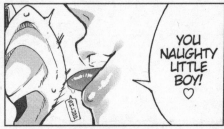

YOU NAUGHTY LITTLE BOY! ♥

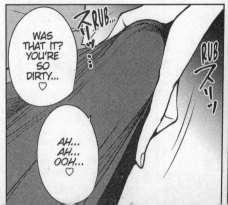

ZU RUB...

WAS THAT IT? YOU'RE SO DIRTY... ♥

RUB ZU...

AH... AH... OOH... ♥

WE'VE GONE THROUGH ALL THIS TROUBLE AND YOU STILL DON'T GET IT?

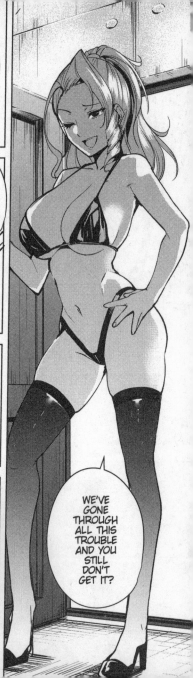

I... DON'T GET IT!!
ARE THEY AFTER MY... VIRGINI-TY?!
SHLURRP
SHLURP
AHN! ♡
AHN! ♡ AHH! ♡
SHLURP
SHLURP
WH... WHAT DOES MY VIRGINITY HAVE TO DO WITH THEM?
YUM... ♡
THIS IS DEFI-NITELY A TRAP.
DRBB
DRBBLLL
I'M SO GONNA GET BLACK-MAILED. BUT... BUT EVEN SO...
MY LIFE ISN'T EXACTLY IN DANGER!
HAH...
HUFF...
HUFF...
THIS IS A DREAM COME TRUE...!

HEE HEE! ♡ MAKE SURE YOU TAKE A GOOD LONG LOOK AT IT GOING IN. ♡
SHOOM
MY VIRGIN RESOLVE IS TESTED! I CAN'T TAKE ANY-MORE!
AH! ♡
TH... THIS IS...
AHH... ♡
SHLIPP
SO HOT...! SO TIGHT...!
THIS IS WHAT A WOMAN FEELS LIKE!
AHH!

HOLY SHIT!! SEX IS ACTUALLY BETTER THAN THE HYPE!
HAHH...
HAHHH...
HAHH...
HAHH...
WA... WAIT...
WHY DID YOU DO THIS?!
WHY TAKE MY VIRGIN-ITY?!
TO SAVE THE WORLD.
CH-CHAK
BLAM

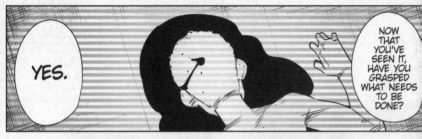

NOW THAT YOU'VE SEEN IT, HAVE YOU GRASPED WHAT NEEDS TO BE DONE?

YES.

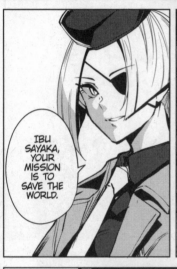

IBU SAYAKA, YOUR MISSION IS TO SAVE THE WORLD.

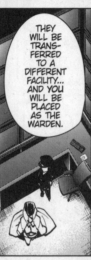

THEY WILL BE TRANSFERRED TO A DIFFERENT FACILITY... AND YOU WILL BE PLACED AS THE WARDEN.

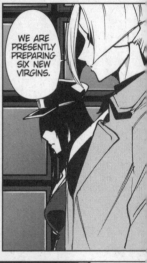

WE ARE PRESENTLY PREPARING SIX NEW VIRGINS.

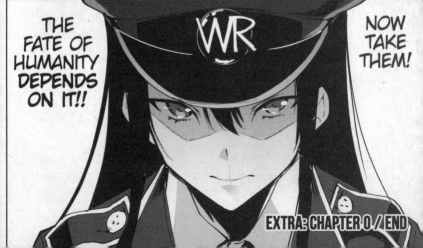

THE FATE OF HUMANITY DEPENDS ON IT!!

NOW TAKE THEM!

EXTRA: CHAPTER 0 / END

DESTINY LOVERS

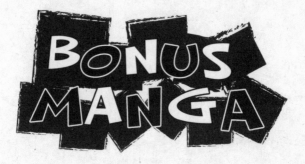

BONUS MANGA

DESTINY LOVERS

03

ドキ
BA-DUM
ドキ
BA-DUM
SU... SUKE-KAWA-SAN... I... I'VE NEVER DONE THIS BEFORE.
D-DON'T BE TOO ROUGH, PLEASE...
CLNNCH
I UNDER-STAND.
SQUISH... くちゅ...
JOLT
ゾク...
...
HAHH!

I... I'M IN...!
GRP TRMBL
TRMBL
DID... I HURT YOU, SAWA?
I... I'M FINE...
I'M GOING TO MOVE NOW.
CLNCH
IT'S SO... WARM...
ズッ... SHFF
AH! ♡
SHWWP
ズリュ...

AHN...
MM...
HAHH♡
AHN...♡
JOLT
AHHH...
AHH...
HAHH...♡
SHLLP
KRIK
KRIK
KRIK
KRIK
AHH...
BA-DUM
AHH...♡
SHPLURT

HAHH...
I'M SORRY, I...
HAHH...
IT'S... OKAY...
HAHH...
I'M SO HAPPY YOU AND I WERE ABLE TO--
MORE.
!!
SUKE-KAWA-SAN... WHAT ARE... THIS IS EMBARA--
GWSSH
IT'S STILL NOT ENOUGH! YOU THINK SO TOO, RIGHT SAWA?!
FWSH
EMBAR-RASSING...

SHLAP
SHLAP
SHLAP
GWOMM
AH! ♡
HAHH...
NO... MORE... ♡
THIS... ♡ I... ♡
SHWIP
SHWIP
KRIK
KRIK
SAWA... MORE... MORE...
SUKE... KAWA ♡ SAN... ♡
KRIIK
AH! ♡
AH! AH! ♡
AHH!! ♡

AH!!
SAWA ...!
SHPLT
SPURT
JOLT
JOLT
HAHH...
HAHH...
HAHH...
MORE...
WHRRRR
MORE!!
END

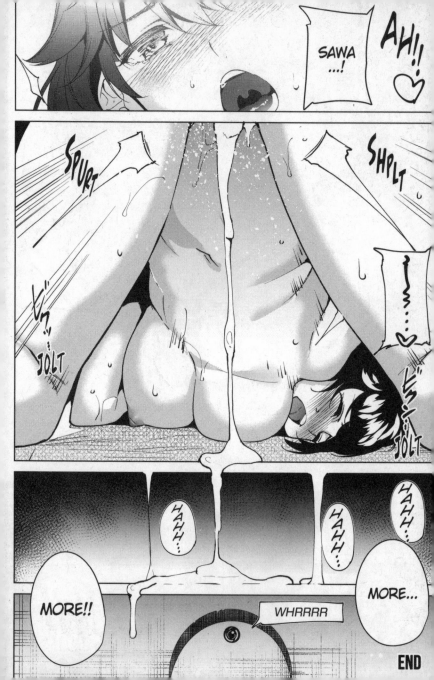

NEXT TIME
DA-DUN
ULTIMATE STRIP ROCK PAPER SCISSORS SHOW-DOWN!
Is this the Last Battle?!
OUT!
SAFE!!
The boys wager their freedom, the girls wager sex...
LET'S PLAY STRIP ROCK PAPER SCISSORS!!
WHY HAVEN'T THEY FORCED US... IN OTHER WORDS, MADE US HAVE SEX WITH THEM?!
Destiny Lovers Volume 4 is coming soon!

SEVEN SEAS' GHOST SHIP PRESENTS

DESTINY LOVERS

story by **KAZUTAKA**　art by **KAI TOMOHIRO**　**VOLUME 3**

TRANSLATION
Thomas Zimmerman

ADAPTATION
Steven Golebiewski

LETTERING AND RETOUCH
Ludwig Sacramento

COVER DESIGN
Nicky Lim

PROOFREADER
Janet Houck

EDITOR
Elise Kelsey

PREPRESS TECHNICIAN
Rhiannon Rasmussen-Silverstein

PRODUCTION MANAGER
Lissa Pattillo

MANAGING EDITOR
Julie Davis

ASSOCIATE PUBLISHER
Adam Arnold

PUBLISHER
Jason DeAngelis

ISBN: 978-1-947804-75-3

Printed in Canada

First Printing: May 2020

10 9 8 7 6 5 4 3 2 1

FOLLOW US ONLINE: *www.ghostshipmanga.com*

READING DIRECTIONS

This book reads from *right to left*, Japanese style.
If this is your first time reading manga, you start
reading from the top right panel on each page and
take it from there. If you get lost, just follow the
numbered diagram here. It may seem backwards at
first, but you'll get the hang of it! Have fun!!

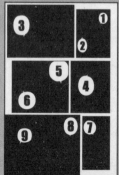